Don Green

AROUND
AFRICA AND ASIA
BY SEA

AROUND AFRICA AND ASIA BY SEA

Adapted from TO THE ENDS OF THE EARTH
by Irene M. Franck and David M. Brownstone

A Volume in the Trade and Travel Routes Series

Facts On File

New York • Oxford • Sydney

Around Africa and Asia by Sea

Facts On File, Inc.	Facts On File Limited	Facts On File Pty Ltd
460 Park Avenue South	Collins Street	Talavera & Khartoum Rds
New York NY 10016	Oxford OX4 1XJ	North Ryde NSW 2113
USA	United Kingdom	Australia

Library of Congress Cataloging-in-Publication Data

Around Africa and Asia by sea: adapted from To the ends of the earth
    by Irene M. Franck and David M. Brownstone.
        p.   cm. — (Trade and travel routes series)
    Bibliography: p.
    Includes index.
    Summary: A historical survey of the Spice Route and the Cape of
    Good Hope Route, used to go around Africa and to reach Asia by sea.
    ISBN 0-8160-1875-8
    1. Trade routes—History—Juvenile literature. [1. Trade routes—
    History.] I. Franck, Irene M. To the ends of the earth. II. Series.
    HE328.A76 1990
    382'.09—dc20   89-11997

British and Australian CIP data available on request from Facts On File.

Facts On File books are available at special discounts when purchased in bulk quantities for businesses, associations, institutions, or sales promotion. Please contact the Special Sales Department of our New York office at 212/683-2244 (dial 800/322-8755 except in NY, AK or HI).

Jacket design by Catherine Hyman
Composition by Facts On File, Inc.
Manufactured by R. R. Donnelley & Sons
Printed in the United States of America

10 9 8 7 6 5 4 3 2 1

This book is printed on acid-free paper.

CONTENTS

LIST OF MAPS

PREFACE

Around Africa and Asia by Sea is one volume in the Trade and Travel Routes series. The series itself is based on our earlier work, *To the Ends of the Earth*, published by Facts On File, Inc. in 1984. This adaptation of the work for young readers has been prepared by Facts On File; many new illustrations have also been added.

Several publishers gave permission to reprint selections from their works. In this volume, the excerpts on pp. 34-36 are from Marco Polo's *The Travels*, translated by Ronald Latham, published by Penguin in 1958, copyright © Ronald Latham, 1958. The maps, drawn from *To the Ends of the Earth*, are by Dale Adams.

Irene M. Franck
David M. Brownstone

INTRODUCTION

WHAT IS A TRADE ROUTE?

In a world without airplanes, engine-powered ships, trucks, or even paved roads, how did people journey from one place to another? How did products that were found only in a very small part of the world eventually find their way across the continents? For almost five thousand years, people have been bringing products from one part of the world to another using trade routes. Traders from Europe, Asia, and Africa carried furs, spices, silks, pottery, knives, stone utensils, jewels, and a host of other commodities, exchanging the products found in one area for the products found in another.

When trading first began, there were no real roads. Local traders might follow trails or cross steep mountain passes in their treks from one village to another. With the passage of time, tracks might be widened and eventually paved. But the new paved roads tended to follow the old trade routes, establishing these routes as important links of communication between different cultures.

As technology advanced, sea-lanes became vital trade routes between the various continents, and made possible trade with North America, South America, and Australia. Many of the highways and seaways that have been used predominantly for trade throughout history have shaped its course of events because of the many ways in which the routes have been used.

WHY STUDY TRADE ROUTES

Studying the trade routes is one way of learning about the history of the world. As we look at the trade routes of Europe, for example, we can see how the nations of that continent have changed throughout the centuries: we learn how Scandinavian Vikings came to sail south and west to settle in France and Britain; we can appreciate how present-day Hungary was originally settled by a wandering tribe from the Ural Mountains, etc. In a similar way, by looking at the trade routes of Africa, we can trace the history of the slave trade and learn about the European colonization of Africa in the 18th and 19th centuries.

In addition, studying the trade routes helps us better understand the origin of many of the institutions and services with which we are familiar today. Postal systems, tolls, guidebooks, roadside restaurants and hotels all came into being, either directly or indirectly, because of trade routes. Studying the trade routes will help you to understand how they emerged.

How to Use This Book

This book is organized in chapters. Each chapter is devoted to the history of one trade route, or in some cases, where the particular trade route has an especially long and eventful past, to a particular era in a trade route's history. Therefore, you can simply read about one trade route that particularly interests you or, alternatively, read about all the trade routes in a given area. At the end of each chapter, you will find a list of books for further reading, which will assist you in locating additional sourcebooks should you need them to support report research or classroom work. If you are using these books as references for a particular history course, check the index of each to find the subject or person you need to know more about. The list of maps at the front of this book will direct you to all maps contained herein, and thereby help you to locate each trade route on the face of the earth.

Studying trade routes can be a fascinating way of learning about world history—and of understanding more about our lives today. We hope you enjoy all the volumes in the TRADE AND TRAVEL ROUTES series.

1

THE SPICE ROUTE: THE EARLY YEARS

THE ROUTE THAT LINKED THE WORLD

From the earliest times in human history, people have been curious about other peoples and other lands. They have wanted to trade with foreign farmers and artisans, to know the people who grew the food and made the goods that were wonderful and strange.

One of the ways that people found to link their different cultures is a pattern of sea voyages that became known as *The Spice Route*.

At its height, the Spice Route linked the great civilizations of the Mediterranean, India, and Southeast Asia. Even people from northern European countries depended on the Spice Route to get the spices, jewels, silks, and other goods that came from the East.

The Shape of the Spice Route. The Spice Route was not one single sea lane. Rather, it was like a spider's web— a network of criss-crossing routes that tied together many places on the western and eastern parts of the Indian Ocean and the Arabian Sea. Many different goods traveled from one place to another along this web.

The western part of the Spice Route started with the Red Sea and the Persian Gulf, on both sides of the Arabian Peninsula. The eastern part of the Spice Route ran from China and from the east coast of Africa, going as far south as the island of Madagascar. All the strands of the Spice Route crossed the Arabian Sea. They all came together at the tip of the Indian Peninsula, between India and the island of Ceylon (now Sri Lanka).

1

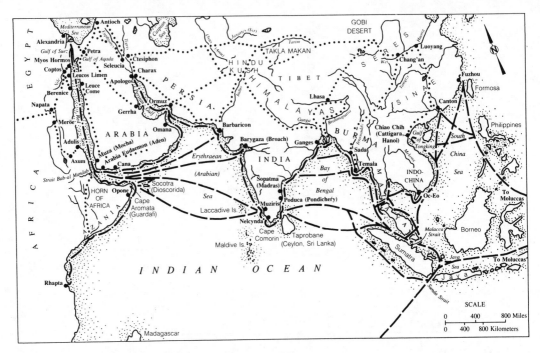

The Spice Route in Greco-Roman Times

——·——·—— Early Sea Routes

——— ——— Sea Routes in Roman Times

· · · · · · Main Connecting Land Routes

⊨ Main Portages

The Spice Route linked together many different countries in its web of trade. The eastern part of the route connected China, Indochina (the part of Southeast Asia that includes today's countries of Laos, Kampuchea, and Vietnam), and the many islands of the Malay Archipelago (the East Indies).

This important route also took in the islands of Sumatra and Java, which today are part of Indonesia.

Sailing on the Spice Route. How could early sailors make the long treks between different continents? What made it possible was the Indian Ocean's pattern of *monsoon winds.*

Monsoons are powerful winds that occur in certain seasons. In the Indian Ocean, the monsoons change direction twice a year, providing a steady northeast wind during winter and a reliable—though sometimes too strong—southwest wind during summer and early autumn. These winds allowed even early sailors in primitive vessels to travel far over the seas and then back home again.

Trade Along the Spice Route. The Spice Route included much trade in spices, which grew in southeastern Asia. The Spice Route was named for the Spice Islands, a group of Malaysian islands also called the Moluccas. However, spices and other luxuries came from many other parts of southeastern Asia as well.

These precious spices were traded to buyers from the western part of the route. Western traders might buy spices with gold and silver. Or the spice traders might go to Africa and trade for ebony, ivory, and human slaves.

The History of the Spice Route. The Spice Route has a long and complicated history, beginning many thousands of years B.C. It began almost as soon as people discovered how to sail the ocean in their frail ships, and continued through the great days of the empires of Rome, China, Arabia, and Srivijaya, on into the days when the European countries controlled many of the countries of Asia and Africa.

Spice trees like these attracted traders for thousands of years. (From de Bry, *Petits Voyages*, Part IV, Frankfurt, 1601)

The story of the Spice Route is the story of shifts in the world economy. The history begins when people lived in isolated countries, linked only by infrequent trade by land or by sea. It continues through the times when empires controlled large sections of land and even sea. Finally, the history concludes in modern times, as one by one, countries of Africa and Asia threw off outside control to become truly independent.

A Historical Detective Story. The Spice Route dates back over 5,000 years. It goes back to a time when many cultures had not developed writing systems, or, if they had, did not keep very detailed records. What evidence or clues exist that would tell us about where the people of that time traveled?

Historians of that early time have to be something like detectives. They have to use clues—the facts we do have—and put them together to tell a convincing story about what happened.

The historian-detectives get help from other scholars. *Archaeologists* examine the past through studying physical objects and *artifacts* that go back many years. Pots, ruins of buildings, graves, tombstones, kitchen utensils, and many other artifacts have been found buried or hidden in different parts of the world. Archaeologists look at these objects and try to figure out what they can about who used them and how they lived.

The study of *linguistics* is another part of the detective's work. Linguistics is the study of languages. By looking at the many different languages spoken all over the world, historians and linguists can figure out which groups of people were related in history or knew each other. For example, if a word from one language turns up in another language, that suggests that the people who spoke the two languages had made contact at some time.

The Sumerians. One thing that historians have discovered is that the Sumerian people from the city of Ur were trading with various ports along the Persian Gulf 5,000 years ago. The city of Ur was located in Mesopotamia, along the Euphrates River, which runs through the modern nations of Syria and Iraq. Based on artifacts found at the various sites, archaeologists have deduced that the Sumerians of Ur traded with at least three different Persian Gulf ports.

Historians also imagine that the traders of Ur dealt with a place called Melukkha, in the Indus Valley, in India. They came to this conclusion because they know that teak—a kind of hardwood which does not occur naturally near Ur—was used in the buildings of Ur as early as 3000 B.C. Teak was abundant along the Malabar Coast of Southwest India. So historians reasoned that the people of Ur got the teak by trading with India.

The Egyptians. The Egyptians were also early long-distance traders. They did keep records, in the form of a kind of picture-writing known as *hieroglyphics*. Once archaeologists had worked out how to read this ancient writing, they were able to decipher the ancient Egyptian records.

Apparently, the Egyptians traded with a land called *Punt*. Historians have not yet been able to figure out exactly where this land is. They have guessed that it was probably in East Africa or southwest Arabia.

At first, Egyptians traded overland with Punt, a trade that was old by 2800 B.C. Then the Egyptians decided to bypass the land route and send expeditions right down the Red Sea. Egyptian records claim that the idea of trading with Punt was of divine origin:

> a command was heard from the great throne, an oracle of the god himself, that the ways of Punt should be searched out, that the highways to the terraces of *'ntyw* [probably myrrh or frankincense, which are fragrant woods] should be penetrated.

In addition to *'ntyw*, Egyptians also brought home ebony, ivory, gold, and two kinds of incense.

Queen Hatshepsut's expedition to the land of Punt was commemorated on a relief near Thebes in the second century B.C., the basis for this drawing. (Authors' archives)

Cinnamon: The Precious Spice. At some point in the next thousand years, the Egyptians began receiving goods that were native only to India or to places farther east. By finding evidence of these goods in Egypt, historians have deduced that the Egyptians were somehow trading with India and other eastern countries.

One of the most important goods to arrive in Egypt from the east was *cinnamon*. This spice, which today can easily be bought at the grocery store, was for many thousands of years the most precious of all the rare spices. It grows only in a few warm countries. The Egyptians valued it because they used it in their practice of *embalming*—the preservation of dead bodies that was part of their religion.

Language Clues. Historians have another clue about Egyptian trade. The Egyptian names for several special items—including peacocks, cinnamon, apes, rice, and sandalwood—came from the Tamil dialects of southern India. If Egypt had been conducting an overland trade with India, we would expect that they would have gotten goods from the northern part of the subcontinent. Because several words in Egyptian are of *southern* Indian origin, we imagine that the Egyptians were trading by sea. Apparently, southern

Birds and fish sometimes guided early sailors on their way across uncharted oceans. (From de Bry, *Petits Voyages*, 1601)

In boats like this one off Southeast Asia, some Malayans may have reached East Africa before the time of Christ. (From G. Waldo Browne, *The New America and the Far East*, 1901)

Arabians acted as middlemen, trading with the Egyptians at one end and the Indians at the other, moving goods—and language—gradually along the Spice Route.

EARLY SAILORS AND THEIR SHIPS

Imagine what it must have been like to have invented ships to travel on the ocean. Today it is easy to ride or even fly over the water. But for many thousands of years, people depended on frail boats that they had built with their own hands to carry them over uncharted seas into foreign lands.

The early peoples of Arabia, Egypt, and Mesopotamia did not even have much wood for building ships. Nor did they have any metal that was good for making nails. Instead, they used reed boats or raft-like craft built of inflated animal skins stretched over small pieces of precious wood.

Later, these peoples imported wood from other places, and used a type of string to tie the logs together. Even into modern times, Arabian boats were generally sewn, rather than nailed together.

Indian sailors had an easier time. They had ready supplies of hardwoods. These were good for use in tropical waters, which caused most other woods to rot quickly.

Europeans and Asians alike would struggle for the port of Ormuz (today called Hormuz), which controlled the strait at the mouth of the Persian Gulf. (Authors' archives)

Even so, the earliest vessels were not strong enough to stand up well against rough seas. In their trading journeys, they usually hugged the coastline.

Dangers and Hardships. It is no wonder that these early sailors did not venture out into the ocean, for the Red Sea and the Persian Gulf were difficult to navigate. Fresh drinking water was scarce, even if ships traveled along the coastline, for much of the coast was desert. Imagine sailing for several days in sight of land, and still not being able to find any water to drink!

The Red Sea also has dangerous coral reefs. A reef is a huge accumulation of the hard skeletons of tiny marine animals. It looks very beautiful, and the reddish or pinkish coral is used to make jewelry. But a coral reef can be like a huge impenetrable wall. Rough waves could send ships crashing into a reef. Reefs are especially dangerous when they are not visible along the surface of the water—but tall enough to catch the bottoms of boats that pass over them.

Also, a north wind blows over the Red Sea all year long. Any ship sailing in the opposite direction would have had quite a hard time. The stories of sailors shipwrecked on the Red Sea go back 4,000 or 5,000 years.

THE FIRST SUEZ CANAL

The Suez Canal is a waterway that connects the Mediterranean Sea with the Gulf of Suez and the Red Sea. Almost 4,000 years ago, however, the Egyptians built a channel connecting the Red Sea with one arm of the Nile River. This channel formed a short-cut and meant that goods could travel by water a much longer distance without the cost of loading and unloading goods traveling by land.

This early "Suez Canal" was 30 miles long and was in use for centuries. Queen Hatshepsut sent a famous expedition to Punt by way of this canal.

However, the canal tended to become choked with silt deposited by the yearly overflowing of the Nile, making it too shallow for ships to use. Some traders preferred to go partway by land to avoid potential trouble on the canal.

INDIAN SAILORS

The sailors who traveled along the Spice Route most frequently in this early period were the Indians. Once again, much of what we know of them has been put together like a detective story. The clues in this case were poems and religious works. These works cannot be easily dated. They were not meant to be accurate historical records. Historians have had to make lots of guesses from little bits of information.

The Vedas. The early religious writings of the Indians are called the *Veda*, which means "knowledge." The Vedic writings are the first holy books of the *Hindu* religion.

Hinduism actually consists of a number of different sects that follow different customs in different parts of India. All of these sects believe that individual souls are constantly *reincarnated*, or born again into different bodies, with the circumstances in their new life depending on how they behaved in their previous life. Their goal is to free themselves from this cycle to achieve union with God, which they believe can be done through *yoga*, spiritual practices leading to knowledge of reality and oneness with God.

One of the early Vedic writings was called the *Rig Veda*. It concerns us because it describes in some detail the building of the Indians' ships. Like Arab ships, they were sewn together. They were colorfully decorated with paintings, animal sculptures, precious metals, and gems.

Clearly, some of these boats were used for royal pleasure trips. But most were used for trade and transport of goods. Some were used as warships, in naval warfare among the many rival Indian kingdoms.

Some of the early religious writings describe ships that held 500 to 800 people. Perhaps these high numbers are exaggerated. Nevertheless, these ships were clearly large and strong enough to withstand the winds of the open seas. Although metal was available, the early shipbuilders chose to construct them entirely without nails.

Daring Deeds of Indian Sailors. These brave early sailors had their own means of navigation. They used birds. When they wanted to know where land was, they would free one of the many birds they carried with them on board ship. The bird would head for land—and the ship would follow.

Indians seem to have been the first Spice Route sailors to risk the open waters. We know this from other religious writings, the *Jatakas*, which are from the *Buddhist* religion. Buddhism is another great eastern religion that began in India. It teaches the practice of meditation, and the idea of following certain moral rules to achieve a noble life. In its earliest history, Buddhism was also concerned with how human beings could become free of human suffering by learning how to become free of all desire.

The *Jatakas*, describing the period between 1000 B.C. and 500 B.C., tell of merchants crossing the Bay of Bengal to trade with the land they called "The Golden Land." The Golden Land, or Suvarnabhumi, is occupied now by the country of Burma and the Malay Peninsula.

The *Sankha-Jataka* describes one Indian who had given away so much of his money to charity that he was sailing to the Golden Land to gain new wealth According to the story in this book, his ship sprang a leak in mid-ocean and he was saved by a magic ship, with "three masts made of sapphire, coradage of gold, silver sails, and...also...[gold] oars and...rudders."

SETTLERS ON THE SPICE ROUTE

To understand these early days on the Spice Route, it is necessary to picture a world where nations and peoples were constantly changing. Trade routes made possible migration from one land to another. In fact, over the thousands of years of human history, the map of the world kept changing. Different languages, cultures, and political boundaries arose, became influential, and then declined. This process continues even today.

Turn your mind back, then, to the thousand years before the birth of Jesus. During this *millennium* (thousand-year period), the Indians began to move eastward.

Actually, at that time, there was no one country of "India." Rather, there were many different countries in the territory that today we call "India"—and some of the peoples of these countries were heading east.

Indian Settlers. The kingdom of Kalinga, on India's east coast, extended even further east to include the island of Ceylon (today called Sri Lanka). Then the Kalingan people, or Klings, began to settle in the Golden Land. They went all the way to the area that is now called Singapore, at the tip of the Malay Peninsula.

The Klings were looked down upon and even persecuted, partly because they practiced Buddhism while others practiced the Hindu religion. Nevertheless, they continued to settle to the east.

This Indian-Malayan ship and its busy crew are sharply outlined on this wall sculpture, called a *bas-relief*. (From Borobudur, Java, eighth century A.D.)

Chinese Settlers. In China, there was little sailing activity until the 4th century B.C., when the Chinese first set out into the open seas. By the third century B.C., they had ventured across the sea to Japan.

In the next century, they took the city of Chiao Chih, which today is the Vietnamese city of Hanoi with its port, Haiphong.

For several centuries afterward, Chinese merchants continued to depend on Chiao Chih for foreign trade, even though this city actually belonged to another people, the Vietnamese. The Chinese also depended on Nanhai (modern Canton, also known as Guangzhou) for foreign trade. But there they stopped. For several centuries, they waited in Chiao Chih for foreign traders—mostly Indians living in Malaya—to bring goods to them.

Arabian Settlers. What was happening in Arabia, on the western end of the Spice Route, is not quite clear. We do know that Southwest Arabia had long been a prime producer of aromatic spices, particularly frankincense, balsam, and myrrh. Over a land route called the *Incense Road*, Arabians traded these products and eastern goods with Egypt and other nearby countries on the Mediterranean.

Several centuries before the birth of Christ, Arabs also began to spread across the water to settle in Africa. They moved across the dangerous Strait of Bab al-Mandab (also known as the Gate of Tears), to the Horn of Africa, the part of the continent occupied by present-day Somalia.

The Arabs moved around the Horn to settle on the East African coast. To some extent, they mixed with local people, but often, they kept to themselves. They set up their own trading settlements and coastal colonies, going as far south as the modern city of Dar Es Salaam.

We know that from both East Africa and South Arabia, the Arabs traded Eastern goods with Egypt and with the Mediterranean lands. What we do not know is whether Arabs were actually sailing on the Spice Route. They may have acted mainly as middlemen, receiving goods supplied by Indian sailors and traders and passing them along.

Cinnamon: A Clue to the Story. Historians have used what we know about cinnamon to try to piece together the story of the early Arabs and Indians. Cinnamon, the queen of all spices, was the most expensive and sought-after spice of early times. It is native to only a few places in Southeast Asia.

For thousands of years, the Egyptians used cinnamon for various purposes, including the practice of embalming. Mediterranean records say again and again that East Africa was "cinnamon-land"—the place where traders found the fabulous spice.

But cinnamon cannot grow in East Africa. So more than one historian has guessed that Indian traders must have sailed across the ocean to bring the precious spice to Arabs on Africa's East Coast. These Arabs in turn took the spice by a land route up to the Nile Valley in Egypt, from where it could be traded to Mediterranean sailors. The Arab traders were careful to keep secret the real place where they had gotten the spice!

Some historians have even guessed that the people of Malaya brought the cinnamon to Africa by sailing directly across the ocean. The Roman writer Pliny said that men of great bravery brought it "over vast seas on rafts." Perhaps he was referring to Malayans and their outrigger canoes, which were something like modern catamarans—two rafts or canoes joined together, floating under a single sail.

Imagine riding such a tiny boat from the modern country of Malaysia (located on the Malay Peninsula) across the ocean to the east coast of Africa! These brave sailors may have reached even as far down the African coast as Madagascar. How do we know that? Well, the language spoken there was, reportedly, similar to the language of the Indians who lived in Malaysia.

THE GREEKS

Alexander the Great. The next great interest in the Spice Route was shown by the Greek leader Alexander the Great.

Alexander was the king of Macedon, a region that today is shared by the countries of Greece, Yugoslavia, and Bulgaria. His tutor was the famous Greek scientist and philosopher Aristotle.

Alexander was a great soldier. He ascended the throne of Macedon in 336 B.C., and by 334 B.C. had managed to conquer all of Greece. Then he moved east, in an effort to conquer the entire known world for the Greeks.

In fact, he managed to conquer a good part of it, including the Persian Empire and Egypt. In Egypt, he founded the port-city that was named for him, *Alexandria*. By 326 B.C. Alexander's empire extended from Greece eastward to northern India. There his men would go no further.

Eventually, Alexander had to retreat. He died in 323 B.C. at the age of 33.

Alexander and the Spice Route. While Alexander was building his empire across three continents, he dreamed of uniting it with trade routes. In northern India, he gathered and built hundreds of ships on the Indus River and sent the fleet to explore the Persian Gulf.

Alexander's action was a lucky one for historians, at least, for the expedition's leader, Nearchus, left the earliest surviving sailor's account of the Persian Gulf. And Alexander's biographer, Arrian, leaves us a valuable record of what the Greeks thought about this "new" ocean. The adventures on it showed them that it was quite different from their familiar Mediterranean!

> In this foreign sea there live great whales and other large fish, much bigger than in our Mediterranean. Nearchus tells us of his encounter with them as follows:

This Spice Route sailor is being rescued not only from drowning but also from the jaws of a fearsome shark. (From Borobudur, Java, eighth century A.D.)

"As we set sail we observed that in the sea to the east of us, water was blown aloft, as happens with a strong whirlwind. We were terrified and asked our pilots what it was and whence it came. They replied that it was caused by whales, which inhabit this sea. Our sailors were so horrified that the oars fell from their hands.

I went and spoke to them encouragingly. Then I walked round the fleet and ordered every steersman I met to steer straight at the whales, exactly as if they were going into a naval battle. All the men were to row hard and with as much noise as possible, including yells. The sailors regained their courage, and at a signal we all set off together. When we had approached the beasts, everyone shouted as loudly as they could. On top of that, trumpets were blown and the noise of the oars echoed across the sea. The whales, which could be seen just in front of the ships, dived terrified into the depths. Not long after, they surfaced again behind the fleet, blowing water into the air as before. The sailors clapped their hands, rejoiced in their escape, and praised Nearchus for his courage and astuteness."

THE EGYPTIANS

Alexander's expedition did not have any significant effect on trade along the Spice Route.

Later, however, the lands at the head of the Red Sea, especially Egypt, were taken over by one of Alexander's heirs, *Ptolemy*. He and his successor, also named Ptolemy, made the Greek city of Alexandria, at the mouth of the Nile River, a major trading and manufacturing center.

All the goods of the East could be found in Alexandria. And while the native Egyptians continued to live along the Nile itself, Greek overlords began to develop the Red Sea trade. The Ptolemies once again reopened the old Egyptian canal at the Gulf of Suez, as well as built new overland routes.

While they were in power, the Ptolemies shipped many items from the East African coast up the Red Sea. There they were unloaded at *caravan* ports, from which overland caravans would take them further west. (A caravan is a group of travelers or merchants that bands together for the sake of helping and defending each other when crossing unsettled or hostile country.) One of the most famous imports was the great African elephant. In the ancient world, those elephants were used like tanks, to carry heavy military equipment and to make fierce attacks. These elephants rivaled the Indian elephants kept by the Seleucid people in Persia.

If we really want a sense of what it was like to sail the Spice Route in the first century B.C., we can look at the guidebooks written for sailors at the time. One of the most interesting works is *Periplus of the Erythraean [Red] Sea*, a practical handbook written by an anonymous Greek merchant-sailor.

The *Periplus* (*periplus* is ancient Greek for "sea voyage around") describes the main ports and routes on the Red Sea, Egypt being the point of departure. The trip was by no means easy. The *Periplus* tells us that the Red Sea was "without harbors, with bad anchorages, foul, inaccessible because of breakers and rocks, and terrible in every way."

When sailors finally reached ports along the Persian Gulf or the Indian coast, they depended on local pilots, who guided the foreign ships into port. Only local pilots who knew the area well could manage the dangerous navigation.

Hugging the Coast. We can also read that for Western sailors (Greeks, Egyptians, Arabs, and others on the west side of the Arabian Sea), the standard route for Egyptian and Arab sailors was to hug the coast, creeping from port to port while staying as close to land as possible. The Arabs especially did not dare to venture onto the open seas in their frail boats.

Braving the Ocean. The Greek sailors did eventually learn how to use the monsoons of the Indian Ocean. They left the coast and let the winds blow them straight across to India. Then, when the season changed, the winds would blow them back again. Of course, Indian sailors had probably been using those winds for centuries. But the Greeks first learned to use them in 45 A.D.

As Western sailors reached farther down the Indian peninsula, other ports on the Malabar Coast came into heavy use. The port of Muziris (later called Cranganore) was described by a Tamil (south Indian) poet:

> The thriving town of Muziris [is] where the beautiful large ships of the Yavanas [Greeks], bringing gold, come splashing the white foam on the waters...and return laden with pepper.

African Trade. The *Periplus* also described the East African coast, where a native population "of very great stature" lived. Goods taken out of Africa included ivory (from elephants' tusks), rhinoceros horn, and palm oil. Here again, the goods that were traded tell us something about the history of the region: the palm oil came from coconut palm trees, brought to Africa by the Indians who had come to settle there many centuries ago.

The *Periplus* also tells about a more cruel kind of trade, the trade in human beings. Slave trade would continue for several more centuries on the Spice Route, as people from Africa were captured and shipped to work as slaves in different parts of the world.

Ptolemy's Mistakes. Western traders may have been familiar with part of the Spice Route, but the part of the route east of the Ganges River in India was a mystery to them. The Roman geographer Ptolemy (not to be confused with the Greco-Egyptian rulers) had made several mistakes in describing the shape of East Asia lands. His mistakes went unrecognized by generations of Westerners. It was not until several centuries later that Western sailors would explore the East and learn its true geography for themselves.

India Expands Its Influence

Although there was some Chinese and Japanese engaged in trade, too, Indians carried on most of the trade on the eastern part of the Spice Route.

India was expanding its religious and political influence as well. Merchants and missionaries carried Indian culture and religion—especially Buddhism—to many parts of Southeast Asia. They were often followed by Indian rulers seeking political control. These rulers usually gained power by peaceful means, without resorting to military conquest.

Greater India. By the first century A.D., there were several Indian-influenced states in Southeast Asia, especially on the Malay Peninsula, in the Mekong River delta in what is now southern Kampuchea, and in the Malay Archipelago. Together these states were known as "Greater India."

The Malay Peninsula required sea travelers to make a 1,000-mile detour around its tip. This was a dangerous area, with many storms—as well as with marauding pirates.

To avoid these dangers, traders often preferred *portage*, to drag or carry their boats and their goods overland, across the peninsula to the water on the other side. Several different portage routes were developed, each controlled by a different kingdom.

Two Great Empires

For a long time, sea trade on the eastern end of the Spice Route was modest. Then two great trading nations arose, one in the East and the other in the West.

The Chinese Empire. In the East, the Han dynasty emerged in China in 202 B.C. Under the Han dynasty, which lasted 400 years, China became a stronger, more unified nation whose merchants were ready to trade with the West.

The Roman Empire. In the West, the Roman Empire was approaching its greatest height. Rome had begun as a tiny city on the Tiber River in Italy. This city grew into an empire first with the conquest of Italy, then huge portions of Europe, the Near East and North Africa.

Between China in the East and Rome in the West lay the overland route called the Silk Road. This was controlled by middlemen from *Parthia*, an ancient Asia country, which by 100 B.C. had grown into an empire extending from the Euphrates to the Indus River.

The Parthians charged heavy tolls and kept foreigners off their trade routes. Therefore, much of the expanding trade between Rome and China was by sea, along the Spice Route.

Indians in the Middle. The Indians made the most of their central position on the Spice Route. Greco-Roman and Arab traders came to the Malabar Coast to buy goods that Indians had collected from the East. Sea trade became so important to the Indian economy that their government appointed a superintendent of ships.

This official was in charge of the whole Indian shipping operation. He built ships with money supplied by the government. He trained sailors to navigate, saw to the collection of port dues, and enforced habor regulations.

Each port also had a superintendent. He was told to lend "the protecting hand of a father" to any battered, storm-weary ships arriving in his harbor.

The Indians also welcomed the ships with *lighthouses*, tall towers with beacons of light on top, to help light up the harbors for ships so that they could avoid being shipwrecked on dark or cloudy nights. Indian lighthouses were built of brick and mortar, and were well known throughout their world.

Traders from Many Lands. The Indian ports saw goods and traders from many parts of the world. A contemporary Indian writer described the mix of wares:

> Horses were brought from distant lands beyond the seas; pepper was brought in ships; gold and precious stones came from the northern mountains; sandal and aghil [aromatic woods] came from the mountains towards the West; pearls from the Southern seas, and coral from the Eastern seas.

Western traders were welcome in Indian ports—but they were confined to separate quarters.

Roman Money. Looking at the money in use along the Spice Route tells us something about the kind of trade that was going on. The Roman gold coin, the *aureus*, and the silver coin, the *denarius*, became the standard currency along the Spice Route.

The fact that Roman money was used tells us that Rome was dominant in Indian trade on the Spice Route. But apparently the Indians also admired the fact that Roman coins all had the same weight, even though they had been coined by many different emperors. (Each emperor put his own portrait on the money he minted—a tradition we carry on today in honor of our leaders.)

The use of one standard type of currency tells us that there were many different peoples and countries involved in trading. Therefore, traders needed one kind of money against which to measure the value of all others. The coins used in any one period indicated who was the dominant country at that time.

The Decline of Arab Traders. Formerly, trading on the western end of the Spice Route had been carried on by the Arabs. Now the Romans were more active, and Arab activity gradually declined.

Western Colonies in India. As Westerners became more active, some Western traders actually settled in India. These included Jews, Armenians, and Syrians. Some of these groups set up colonies that lasted into the 20th century. The Jewish settlement in Cochin, India, for example, was active until well after World War II.

The Decline of Rome. Gradually, the Roman Empire shifted its center from the west to the east. The capital of the empire was no longer Rome (in modern Italy), but Constantinople (today called Istanbul, in modern Turkey). Sixty years later, in 395, the Roman Empire was permanently divided.

As the Western Roman Empire lost strength, new countries sent their traders to profit from the spice trade. From the East African region of Ethiopia, a mixed Arab and African people formed the kingdom of *Axum*. Through their port of Adulis, they came to supply the Mediterranean lands with all the goods of the Spice Route. However, Alexandria, in modern Egypt, was still the main trading port that connected the Spice Route with Europe.

Persian Activity. In the 3rd century, the Persian Empire revived under the Sassanid dynasty. The Persians took control of lands from northern Mesopotamia, almost as far as the Indus River. They also entered the sea trade. With the Arabs leaving the trade and the Persians entering it, the Persian Gulf replaced the Red Sea as the main western end of the Spice Route.

Chola Expands. For all of these traders, the main destination was the Tamil kingdoms of southern India. These kingdoms gradually came under the control of *Chola*, on the southeast coast of India. Chola eventually made the island of Taprobane (Ceylon, now Sri Lanka) into an international trading port. There Axian, Jewish, Syrian, Greek, and Persian traders met Indian and Malay merchants.

INDIAN MIDDLEMEN IN THE FAR EAST

Colonizers and Traders. The eastern end of the Spice Route also saw much growth in the heyday of the Chinese and the Roman empires. The Indians took advantage of their position as middlemen between these two great markets.

Indian traders moved throughout Southeast Asia, setting up protected way stations as far as Vietnam and China. They especially protected the way to the ports of Chiao Chih (now Hanoi-Haiphong, Vietnam), and Nanhai (now Canton, China).

These traders were followed by colonists, rulers, and missionaries, trying to make the region even more "Indian." The island of Java (now part of Indonesia), Champa in central Vietnam, and Funan in southern Kampuchea were all established in the first century A.D.

Traders along these routes were mostly Indian. Europeans rarely went this far east.

Chinese Traders. The Chinese themselves generally waited for others to come to them. But while they waited, they made some forays along the Spice Route. They may even have gone as far as India.

More often, traders met at intermediate ports. The Malay portages—overland travels between sea routes—were popular occasions for the Chinese to meet Indians, who then loaded the Chinese goods into their ships to take to the West.

BEFORE THE EMPIRES AROSE

This, then, is the story for the early days of the Spice Route. Traders from many different lands traveled its many sea-lanes, carrying spices, gold, jewels, ivory, elephants, incense, and many other precious goods. But no one empire controlled any great portion of the route.

In the sixth century, the Spice Route was to enter a new era. From that time on, great empires would control significant parts of the Spice Route, first from the east, then from the west.

2
THE SPICE ROUTE AND THE EMPIRES OF THE EAST

EMPIRES ALONG THE SPICE ROUTE

For the first few thousand years of its history, the Spice Route ran through many different kingdoms and was used by many different peoples, but was never solely under the control of one empire. In the sixth century, this situation was to change. Srivijaya, based on the tiny island of Sumatra (part of present-day Indonesia), was to rise to prominence in Southeast Asia. Srivijaya was to dominate the Spice Route for seven centuries, from the sixth to the 14th century A.D.

Srivijaya was the first empire to take control of a large part of the Spice Route, but it would not be the last. The Chinese and the Arabs also took their turn in controlling the profitable spice trade. Until the end of the 15th century, the Spice Route would be controlled by empires based in the Middle or the Far East. This Eastern control continued until the entrance of the Europeans in 1498.

Chapter 3 of this book tells the story of the European domination of the Spice Route trade. This chapter is concerned with what happened in the eight centuries after the rise of the Eastern empires, before the Europeans came.

By the sixth century, the Roman Empire had lost much of its power. The Chinese Empire, which was then based in the northern part of China, had come under attack from nomads riding out of central Asia. The Middle East and South Asia, however, were mostly untouched by these events. The Spice Route continued to thrive. At this time, a new power arose in the eastern half of the Spice Route—Srivijaya.

Srivijaya's Strategic Position. In the fifth century, Srivijaya had been just one of many small kingdoms in Southeast Asia. Like its neighbors, Srivijaya normally dealt with China through middlemen in *Indochina*—the Southeast Asia region that today includes the countries of Vietnam, Kampuchea (formerly Cambodia), Laos, Thailand, Malaysia, and Burma.

But by the sixth century, several kingdoms, including Srivijaya, began to trade directly with China. Soon Srivijaya assumed control over the other countries in the region. It would hold onto this control for the next seven centuries.

Srivijaya's greatest asset was its location. The island of Sumatra was bordered by two vital Spice Route straits—Malacca and Sunda.

Srivijaya took advantage of this by building a strong navy. That navy sailed into the straits to clear the area of pirates. For the first time, sea routes were safer, cheaper, and easier to take than the land route across Malaya. The new power also improved harbors for merchant sailors.

Tolls for Foreigners. As the navy grew stronger, it began to force all foreign ships to stop at a Srivijayan port and pay *tolls*, or fees for travel. These tolls were in force for centuries. As late as the 12th century, a Chinese writer complained:

> If some foreign ship passing this place should not enter [this port], an armed party would certainly come out and kill [the crew] to the last man.

Pilgrims and Priests. Traders and ambassadors were not the only ones to travel these eastern waters. From the 1st century A.D., Buddhism had spread eastward from India, both overland on the Silk Route and over sea on the Spice Route. Devout Buddhists from as far as China and Japan made *pilgrimages*, or religious journeys, to India.

Sometimes these journeys took several years. Often, pilgrims spent long periods in Buddhist monasteries and universities along the way. Some of these holy places were in Srivijaya.

The seventh-century Chinese Buddhist I-Ching is typical. He studied the Indian language in a Srivijayan city for six months before he went to India, where he spent another 14 years. He recommended that other pilgrims do the same.

> If a Chinese priest wishes to go to the west in order to hear and read, he had better stay here [in Srivijaya] one or two years and practice the proper rules and proceed to Central India.

THE GROWTH OF ISLAM

At the same time that Srivijaya was gaining power, a great religion was arising in the Middle East. In the seventh century, the prophet Mohammed founded a new religion in Arabia— *Islam*. Islam recog-

This mosque in Malacca, shows the spread of the Moslem religion eastward along the Spice Route. (Authors' archives)

nizes Adam, Noah, Abraham, Moses, and Jesus as prophets of God, but holds that Mohammed is the greatest of God's prophets. Mohammed wrote a book called the *Koran*, which the followers of Islam, called *Moslems*, consider holy.

The religion of Islam spread with astonishing speed. At that time, Moslems tended to be militant and proud of their religion, eager to carry Islam into other lands and convert their inhabitants. Within a century, the new religion had spread to all the lands at the far western end of the Spice Route, including Arabia, Mesopotamia, Syria, and Egypt.

As you can see, Islam was practiced in many desert countries. For a few decades, the religion even forbade sailing. Later, the Moslem Arabs in these regions drew on their tradition and experience to become a naval power on the Spice Route.

War with India. During the 800 years between the eighth and the 16th centuries, several Moslem countries were at times at war with India. Yet these land wars did not seriously affect sea trade. Merchant adventurers continued to land and to trade freely in India's rich ports.

Perhaps this freedom was possible because many of the merchants on Arab ships were actually non-Moslems. They were often Greeks (who followed the Greek Orthodox branch of Christianity), Syrians (that is, Christian Syrians), Jews, and Indians (who were either Hindu or Buddhist).

However, Moslem pressure did push many Indians out of western India. Some went to the lands of "Greater India." Others became pirates in the islands of the Arabian Sea.

Throughout this time of change, trading on the Spice Route continued much as it had before. Whatever their ethnic or religious backgrounds, foreign traders were housed in special quarters at distant ports. That way they could be watched and regulated by the host countries.

A New Stability. With Islamic power in the West and Srivijayan power in the East, the Spice Route was safer and more secure than it had ever been before. Pirates gave traders far less trouble, although they still attacked some ships.

After the kingdom of Persia (today's Iran) converted to Islam, the Red Sea and the Persian Gulf were both under Islamic control. Then, since the Persian Gulf had better conditions for sailing, it came to take most of the trade.

Complete with passengers, slaves, and crew, this 12th-century Arab ship sails the Persian Gulf. (Bibliothèque Nationale, Paris)

ARAB-CHINESE RELATIONS

The Arabs Expand. Arab traders did not simply tighten their hold on the Spice Route. They also expanded. By the sixth century, Persian ships were already trading directly with China, mainly through the port of Canton (as the port came to be called in the West). In fact, the Chinese pilgrim I-Ching took a Persian ship from Canton to Srivijaya in 671 A.D. The Moslems built on this base.

Chinese Regulations. The Moslem trade was highly regulated by the Chinese. According to one anonymous Arab author, these regulations gave a good deal of power to the Chinese government:

> When the seamen come in from the sea, the Chinese seize their goods and put them in the sheds; there they guard them securely for [up to]

six months, until the last seaman has come in. After that, three-tenths of every consignment is taken as a duty [tax], and the remainder is delivered to the merchants. Whatever the Government requires, it takes at the highest price and pays for promptly and fairly.

Strained Relations. The Chinese were holding goods for quite a long time—until the last merchant arrived in port for the season. They claimed that their aim was only to provide a fair market, so that no merchant could take advantage of the fact that he might have arrived early.

Of course, this action also served to hold prices down. Imagine how much you might be willing to pay for goods that only one merchant was importing. Now think how much less you would pay for those same goods if you knew you could buy them from any one of 40 merchants! Naturally, merchants did not like these regulations! Chinese records report that in 758, "The Arabs and Persians together sacked and burned the city of Canton and went back by sea." After this violent reaction, the port of Canton was closed for half a century, replaced by the port that today is known as Hanoi-Haiphong.

Moslem Dominance of the Spice Route. Moslem ships were trading from one end of the Spice Route to the other. They celebrated their new power. As one Arab writer put it, "...there is no obstacle between us and China; everything on the sea can come to us."

Once again, the money used tells us something about who controlled trade on the Spice Route. After the fall of Rome in 476, the Persian *dirhem* had been the standard currency all along the route. Now the *dirhem* was replaced by the Arabian *dinar*.

Far-Traveling Merchants. Merchants were traveling farther than ever along the Spice Route. Some seem to have traveled all the way from Europe to China and back again. The ninth-century Arab geographer Ibn Kurdadhbih described the route of some Jewish merchants of his time:

These merchants speak Persian, Roman [Greek and Latin], Arabic, and the Frankish [ancestor of modern French], Spanish, and Slav languages. They travel from West to East and from East to West, sometimes by land, sometimes by sea. From the West they bring back eunuchs, female slaves, boys, silk, furs, and spices. They sail from the country of the Franks [modern France], on the Western Sea [the

Mediterranean], and head towards Farama [near Port Said on the modern Suez Canal]; there they load their goods on the backs of beasts of burden and take the land route to Qulzum [Suez], a five days' journey....They set sail on the East [Red] Sea and make their way from Qulzum to Al Jar and Jidda [in Arabia]; thence they go to Sind [the Indus region], India, and China. On their return they load up with musk, aloes, camphor, cinnamon, and other products of the Eastern countries, and come back to Qulzum, and then to Farama, where they set sail again on the Western Sea. Some head to Constantinople [modern Istanbul] to sell their goods; others make their way to the country of the Franks.

THE EAST AFRICA TRADE

Many Peoples. The Moslems were also active along the East African portion of the Spice Route, where a mixed population of Arabs, Indians, and Africans had lived for many years.

After the founding of Islam, Moslems came to settle on the East African coast. Some of these Moslems were the Omani people, who had tried and failed to form an independent kingdom in eastern Arabia.

Shiites and Sunnis. Other Moslem refugees in East Africa belonged to a minority branch of Islam, called the *Shiites*. Over the centuries many Shiite Moslems sought refuge from their rivals, the *Sunnis*, who were the major branch of Islam, comprising about 85 percent of all Moslems. The division between the Shiites and the Sunnis was caused by disagreement over who should be the successor to Mohammed. They also disagreed over some matters of law and ceremony.

Other Rivalries. Many different peoples had been arriving in East Africa over the centuries, and each brought their rivalries with them. Thus the settlements along the coast were each independent cities, each behind fortified walls. Towns along the coast included Mogadishu, Malindi, Mombasa, Pemba, Zanzibar, Kilwa and Sofala.

Sometimes one city would dominate some of the others. But there was no real empire that controlled all the cities. By the ninth or 10th century all were converted to Islam, but they did not make up an "Arab empire." And though the Arabs ruled on the land, long-time Indian settlers ran the businesses and the ships in the "Arab" coastal trade.

Slave Trading and Slave Revolts.

In East Africa, the main item of Moslem trade was human beings. African slaves sold by the Moslems were sent to Asia, especially Turkey, Arabia, Persia, and India.

So many slaves were sent to Asia that sometimes they were able to revolt. In the mid ninth-century, 400 African slaves taken into the army revolted in Mesopotamia. They eventually took and sacked the city of Basra (now an important port in Iraq), and ruled the region for 14 years.

Six centuries later, in the 15th century, the king of Bengal, a kingdom in India, had 8,000 African slaves. Some of these had actually been promoted into the court. They organized to murder the king, and an African took the throne.

For seven years, Africans ruled Bengal. Some of these African rulers were actually representing the Asian ruler who had inherited the throne. Others were revolutionaries. Finally, all Africans were expelled from the kingdom. After being brought in as slaves, they were exiled as rebels. Some found refuge in western or southern India.

When the Moslems controlled the Spice Route, Yemen was a main slave-trading center. (From al-Hariri, *Maqamat*, 1237, MS. ar. 1847 f. 105, Bibliothèque Nationale, Paris)

This slave trade was a major part of the trade on the western end of the Spice Route in these centuries, and Yemen was one of the main slave trading centers. It does not seem to have extended to China, however. The occasional African slave mentioned in Chinese records is treated as most unusual.

THE CHINA TRADE

Arab-Chinese Relations. China's trading habits during these centuries varied a good deal. Canton had been closed after Arabs and Persians sacked the city to protest Chinese trade regulations. It was reopened in 792, and Arabs and others resumed trade there.

Then, in 878, the city saw more violence. Chinese rebels massacred merchants in Canton's foreign quarter. One Chinese report estimated that 12,000 foreigners were killed. This number may be too high, but whatever the actual number, the event certainly had a chilling effect on Moslem trade in China.

For several centuries after that, Moslem traders went no further than the Malay Peninsula. There they met and traded with merchants from farther east.

Jewish Traders. Some Jewish merchants did continue to trade all the way to China into the 10th century. They generally sailed from the Red Sea, which, with the rise of the rule of the Fatimids in Egypt, had once again become more important than the Persian Gulf.

China, Korea, and Japan. The China Sea also saw some changes. The old main route of trade and influence had been from north China, around to Korea, and across the sea to Japan. But Korea and Japan had suffered bad relations in the eighth century. Thus Japan decided to trade directly across the 500-mile-wide sea to China.

However, in the ninth century, Koreans controlled a triangular trade among the three countries. Many of these Koreans were political exiles from their own country. They set up merchant settlements in China and Japan, going back and forth between the two countries bearing goods.

The Japanese exported metalwork, including superior swords and other weapons. What they wanted in exchange included spices, medicines, and Buddhist artifacts—for the Chinese had already "exported" Buddhism to Japan some time ago.

However, by the end of the ninth century, Buddhism became a weaker force in China. In addition, China saw political turmoil, which decreased trade. Japan was also resisting Chinese influence, and so had less desire to trade.

Trade continued at a low level until the 12th century. By this time, the *Sung* dynasty of southern China had come to power. Suddenly, under the powerful Sung, the Chinese controlled the Far East.

Yet again, money tells us how much influence the Chinese had on trade. Chinese traders were so dominant that in the 13th century Chinese coins were made legal tender in Japan and Japan's mint actually closed down.

THE FALL OF SRIVIJAYA

The Balance of Power Shifts. While the Chinese traders were rising, the Indian traders along the middle of the Spice Route were declining. This shift in the balance of power led to in-fighting among the Indians themselves.

The Rise of the Cholas. The Chola Empire of southern India resented the inroads that Arab traders had made. But they were afraid to attack the Arabs directly. Instead, they attacked the Indian people who had allied themselves with the Arabs. They took much territory from these allies, including the island of Ceylon (Sri Lanka) and the Maldive Islands (in the Indian Ocean southwest of Ceylon), where the Arabs built ships out of Indian teak wood and Maldive coconut fiber.

Turning eastward, the Cholas then confronted the old empire of Srivijaya. In the 10th century, Srivijaya was still a major power along the Spice Route. Its ships were seen from Canton to India. But the Cholas quickly captured the Srivijayan's capital and its major ports.

The Cholas had not really intended to conquer Srivijaya. They only wanted to break that empire's monopoly and go back home. But the war weakened both sides.

New Powers. As a result of this new weakness, new powers arose in the region, especially on the island of Java (in modern Indonesia) and at Malacca (in Malaysia). A traders' colony of many different peoples formed just across the strait from the old Srivijayan capital of Palembang.

New Products. The results were important, for the region and for the Spice Route. With Srivijaya's monopoly broken, the Javanese began to develop products that had not been standard goods on the Spice Route. They began to sell cloves, mace, and nutmeg, which became very popular in the Near East and in Europe. Moslem and Indian merchants moved into the islands as never before, hoping to sell the new products.

New Conversions. With hopes of independence from Srivijaya and plans for gain from the rich Arab trade, many of the smaller kingdoms of the region converted to Islam. As Islam became a more popular religion, Buddhism declined.

The Hindu religion frowned on sea trade. That meant that anyone who wanted to be a trader was more likely to become a Moslem. This helped assure Moslem control both of the Spice Route and of the region.

The Mongols

Moslem ships were not alone on the Spice Route, however. At first, while the Sung dynasty was still in power, Chinese ships had traded as far as India.

Then, in the 13th century, China fell to the Mongols, a people who lived to the north of China in the area that is the present-day country of Mongolia. Thus began the era of the *Yuan* dynasty of the Mogols.

Kublai Khan. The Mongol emperor Kublai Khan destroyed the last of the Sung fleet. Then he had a new navy built. With it, he attacked Japan and parts of Southeast Asia, as far south as Java. But these military ventures were unsuccessful.

Then, at the end of the 13th century, the emperor tried a new tack. He began to use the ships to trade by sea. From 1260 to 1382 the Mongols ruled Asia—and conquered China became a great sea power. Great Chinese ships called *junks* sailed between China and India. Chinese merchants became a common sight along the Malabar Coast.

comptcrons dauters closes.

The famous traveler
Marco Polo returned to
the Mediterranean by
way of the Spice Route.
(Bibliotèque Nationale,
Paris)

In that century, the combination of Mongol control on land and open travel on sea allowed travelers to wander the East as never before. Even some Europeans made their way eastward, to see the land that until then had been a great mystery to them and their people.

Marco Polo. One famous European explorer who helped connect East and West was the Italian voyager Marco Polo. Polo traveled from Venice to China and back again in the 13th century. He described his return trip on a Chinese junk:

> They have one deck; and above this deck, in most ships, are at least sixty cabins, each of which can comfortably accommodate one merchant. They have one steering-oar and four masts; often they add another two masts, which are hoisted and lowered at pleasure. The entire hulk is of double thickness...caulked outside and in, and the fastening is done with iron nails.
>   Some of the ships, that is the bigger ones, have also...partitions made of stout planks dovetailed into one another. This is useful in case the ship's hull should chance to be damaged in some place by striking

on a reef or being rammed by a whale in search of food—a not infrequent occurrence, for if a whale happens to pass near the ship while she is sailing at night and churning the water to foam, he may infer from the white gleam in the water that there is food for him there and so charge full tilt against the ship and ram her, often breaching the hull at some point....

With Marco Polo testing the product, laborers pick the famous pepper from the Malabar Coast. (Bibliothèque Nationale, Paris)

Pirates!

Both Chinese and Moslem sailors had to deal with pirates in the late 13th century. Indeed, some pirates were very well organized. They would leave their island bases in season and fan out along unprotected parts of the Spice Route. Marco Polo described them in the Arabian Sea:

You must know that from Malabar and from a neighboring province called Gujarat [in India], more than 100 ships cruise out every year as corsairs [pirate ships], seizing other ships and robbing the merchants. For they are pirates on a big scale. I assure you that they bring their wives and little children with them. They spend the whole summer on a cruise and work havoc among the merchants. Most of these villainous corsairs scatter here and there, scouring the sea in quest of merchant ships. But sometimes their evil-doing is more concerted. For they cruise in line, that is to say at distances of about five miles apart. In this way twenty ships cover 100 miles of sea. And as soon as they catch sight of a merchant ship, one signals to another by means of beacons, so that not a ship can pass through this sea undetected. But the merchants, who are quire familiar with the habits of these villainous corsairs and know that they are sure to encounter them, go so well-armed and equipped that they are not afraid to face them after they have been detected. They defend themselves stoutly and inflict great damage on their attackers. But of course it is inevitable that one should be captured now and then. When the corsairs do capture a mechant ship, they help themselves to the ship and the cargo; but they do not hurt the men. They say to them: "Go and fetch another cargo. Then, with luck, you may give us some more."

Pirates like these roamed East Asian waters, attacking ships bound for Canton or other ports. (Authors' archives)

For the Chinese, pirates from the Japanese coasts were the worst. They were kept down somewhat during the early Mongol period. Then, when Mogol rule began to decline in the late 14th century, the Japanese pirates rose again.

THE GREAT CHINESE VOYAGES

The Ming Dynasty. After the Yuan dynasty of the Mongols came China's new *Ming* dynasty. Under the Ming dynasty, China reached its greatest height as a sea power. It joined with Japan to put the Japanese pirates down. Under the Ming, China also resumed the old imperial practice of demanding tribute, or payment, from other

With junks like this one, the Chinese would win the Spice Route—and then let it go. (By Manning de V. Lee, in Rupert Sargent Holland, *Historic Ships,* 1926)

countries, in symbolic recognition of Chinese authority. The Ming rulers sent missions throughout Southeast Asia and India, collecting this tribute, which had to be paid for trade with China to continue. Countries eager to trade with China readily accepted to pay tribute.

Cheng Ho and His Voyages. The most famous of these tribute missions were seven great voyages conducted by Cheng Ho. He went far beyond familiar territory, exploring lands that were new to the Chinese. Between 1405 and 1433, his fleets went to the port of Ormuz (modern Hormuz) on the Persian Gulf, then to Aden, which sent a giraffe for the Ming court, and all the way south along the East African coast, well past Mogadishu.

Cheng Ho's fleets had several dozen ships and carried tens of thousands of men. They made China the leading power of the Spice Route, even beyond the Moslems. Cheng Ho himself saw his achievement as contributing to the total power of China:

The countries beyond the horizon and at the ends of the earth have all become subjects; and to the most western of the western or the most northern of the northern countries, however far they may be, the distances of the routes may be calculated....The barbarian countries we have visited are...more than thirty countries large and small. We have traversed more than one hundred thousand *li* of immense water spaces and have beheld in the ocean huge waves like mountains rising sky-high, and we have set eyes on barbarian regions far away hidden in a blue transparency of light vapors, while our sails, loftily unfurled like clouds, day and night continued their course, rapid like that of a star, traversing the savage waves as if we were treading a public thoroughfare.

The Decline of China's Sea Trade. But these voyages did not lead to permanent sea power for China. This was because feeling within the Ming court turned against sea adventures. Those opposed to Cheng's voyages believed China produced all the goods it needed and that foreign goods and influences were dangerous to Chinese society. Indeed, Cheng Ho's records were mostly destroyed, so no one could follow up on his explorations. China had held the chance to control the Spice Route—but had given it up.

THE MOSLEMS REGAIN POWER

After the Chinese turned away from foreign trade, the Moslems once again controlled the Spice Route, continuing trade and travel as they had for centuries. Moslem sailors—many of them Indians sailing with crews of African slaves—were drawing on their old experience as well as discovering new methods of navigation.

The Compass and the Stars. For many years, Moslem sailors had been charting their course by the stars. An experienced navigator could tell where he was by looking at the stars. The Moslem holy book, the *Koran*, noted: "[Allah, or God] hath appointed for you the stars that ye guide yourselves thereby in the darkness of land and sea."

But from the Chinese, the Moslems had learned a new method of navigation—the compass. This device had a needle that was magnetized to respond to the pull of the North or the South Pole. Thus navigators always knew which way was north, or south. The compass meant that even when it was too foggy, too rainy, or too dark to see the stars, sailors could guide their ships.

At this time, however, the compass was still a crude device, and sailors used it only when there was no other way to steer. As one Chinese sailor explained:

This Indian pilot, surrounded by his navigational instruments, was working in a craft thousands of years old in India. (By Thomas Postans, c. 1835, Indian Office Library)

The shipmaster to ascertain his geographic position by night looks at the stars; by day he looks at the sun; in dark weather he looks at the south-pointing needle.

The compass helped sailors guide themselves on the open sea.

Owning, Renting, and Peddling. The merchants on the Spice Route usually made short trips in this period. Most merchants were simply peddlers, traveling on other people's ships with their packs of goods. Some wealthier merchants owned or rented their own ships.

Buddhist and Moslem Pilgrims. Besides traveling merchants, this period also saw pilgrims of many religions taking sea voyages to the places that they considered holy. Some Buddhist pilgrims still voyaged to China, though not as many as in centuries past. But all religious Moslems were supposed to visit their holy city of Mecca (where Mohammed first preached) at least once before they died.

The many Moslem countries of Southeast Asia sent large numbers of pilgrims west along the Spice Route toward Mecca. For many, of course, religion provided an excuse to see the world. In these prosperous times on the Spice Route, many people had a hankering to travel.

Before the Europeans

This chapter describes the activities on the Spice Route up until the end of the 15th century. Although control of the route had shifted between Srivijaya, China, and the Arabs, the route had always been under the control of some power in the region of the route itself.

With the explorations of the Europeans, all that was to change. Soon foreign empires from outside the Spice Route would be dominating these rich lands and their prosperous trade.

3

THE SPICE ROUTE UNDER EUROPEAN CONTROL

THE AGE OF EXPLORERS

For many hundreds of years, the Spice Route was the province of Arabs, Chinese, Africans, and Indians. Some Greek and Roman traders as well as some Jews from various parts of the world might have done some business in the Middle East, in India, or even in China. For the most part, however, the Spice Route was only a concern of those who lived along it.

Then, in 1498, the history of the Spice Route took a turn that would change it forever. That was the year in which the Portuguese explorer Vasco da Gama entered the Spice Route territory, hoping to set up a spice trade for the Portuguese.

Explorers and the Renaissance. The end of the 15th century was a time when all sorts of changes were happening in Europe. Artists were rediscovering the ancient Greek methods of portraying the human body in art, and of using anatomy to show the beauty of the human body. They were using the Greek ideas to explore new ways of painting and sculpting.

At the same time, scientists were challenging centuries of superstition and old beliefs by exploring the world for themselves. They were developing new theories about astronomy, anatomy, and the laws of physics.

Traders and merchants were finding new ways of doing business as well. They were pushing out, looking for new markets and new ways of making money.

Because this was a time of growth and excitement, scholars came to call this period the *Renaissance*, which means "rebirth." Historians saw this period, from the late 15th century through the late 16th century, as a time when knowledge and creativity were being "reborn" after having been ignored for many centuries.

This was the world in which Portugal and other European countries were sending out explorers. These explorers went out to familiarize themselves with foreign cultures and foreign produce in places they had either dim or no knowledge of. The lands they came across—the Americas, the East Indies, Africa, the Far East—had complicated, highly developed cultures of their own, sustained through centuries of trade with neighboring lands. This was especially the case of countries situated on the Spice Route.

THE PORTUGUESE FIND THE SPICE ROUTE

Vasco da Gama. In 1497 Vasco da Gama was sent by King Manuel of Portugal to find a route to India. He was trying to get there by going around the southern tip of Africa, reached by his countryman Bartholomeu Dias in 1488. (See Chapter 4.)

The Portuguese had sent spies to the Near East to learn about the faraway places they wanted to reach. Nevertheless, da Gama and his crew were shocked when they sailed out of the untraveled waters south of Madagascar and stumbled upon the great Moslem cities of the East African coast.

Moslems and Portuguese. Fortunately for the Portuguese, who only six years earlier had helped to expel the Moslem Moors from Spain, the Moslem city-states on the East African coasts were fighting among themselves. The first few ports were hostile to the Portuguese but because the area was not united, the Portuguese were able to find a friendly port, Malindi, where they were welcomed and given an experienced Indian navigator to guide them to Calicut, a city on the Malabar Coast.

Indians and Portuguese. The Portuguese probably considered everyone outside of Europe to be primitive. Ironically, the Indians whom they met were not very impressed with their "higher culture."

The Indians had been trading fine goods for gold and silver for thousands of years. So they found the rough cloth and crude hardware of the Europeans laughable. Some were even insulted that anyone would offer these goods in exchange for their fine silks and ornaments.

The Portuguese, meanwhile, were surprised at the beauty, luxury, and sophistication of Indian civilization. One Portuguese sailor, Duarte Barbosa, described Kilwa, one of the main cities of the region:

> ...[it is] a Moorish town with many fair houses of stone and mortar, with many windows after our fashion, very well laid out in streets, with many flat roofs. The doors are of woods, well-carved, with excellent joinery. Around it are streams and orchards and fruit-gardens with many channels of sweet water....It is a place of great traffic and has a good harbour in which are always moored small craft of many kinds and also great ships....

THE PORTUGUESE TAKE THE SPICE ROUTE

Forcing an Entry. The Portuguese soon saw that they could not compete on the Spice Route on equal terms. In addition to easterners' centuries of experience in this trade, eastern goods were far superior to theirs. They realized that if they wanted entry into the Spice Route trade, they would have to force their way in.

Vasco da Gama went back to Portugal with his sample cargo of peppers and other spices. He showed King Manuel what riches were to be gained from the East. The Portuguese then sent strong fleets to the Cape of Good Hope—the southern tip of Africa. They were ready to show their strength, even to make threats, to get what they wanted.

Portuguese goods might have been crude, but their guns were superior. By 1503, da Gama had collected tribute from Kilwa and bombarded Calicut for its earlier cold welcome. He defeated an even larger Moslem fleet off the Malabar Coast.

Gaining Control. Over the next 10 years, the Portuguese gradually took each of the main East African ports—Sofala, Kilwa, Mombasa, and later, Mozambique. They also took the island ports of Socotra and Ormuz (today, Hormuz).

The Portuguese completely defeated a Moslem army of people from many nations. They also took the shipbuilding island of Goa off Malabar. Then they crossed the Bay of Bengal to take Malacca. From there they reached Canton and the Spice Islands.

In a series of brilliant military moves, the Portuguese had taken all the key points of the Spice Route. Now, they were able to control trade along it. They demanded that each ship traveling through Spice Route waters be "licensed"—that is, that each ship pay "protection money" to the Portuguese. Any ship that did not pay was attacked.

A New Route on the Spice Route. In a relatively short space of time, the Portuguese destroyed the Spice Route as it had been for thousands of years. Before, ships had sailed from China to Egypt and Mesopotamia with goods for the Near East. These goods were then shipped across to Europe by sailors working out of Genoa and Venice in Italy.

Now, the Portuguese took a different route. Goods gathered along the Spice Route no longer went to the Near East. Instead, they followed the Cape of Good Hope Route—around Africa and directly up into the European markets.

Ships from Portugal went first to the rich East African ports, where they could rest from the long journey from Europe. Then, they usually crossed the sea to India, bypassing both the Red Sea and the Persian Gulf. From there, it was on to the Spice Islands and up to Canton—then back to Europe by way of Africa again.

Some old-style trading with the Near East continued. But for the first time in history, the western end of the Spice Route became a backwater. Europeans had pushed Egypt, Persia, Mesopotamia, and Arabia from the center of world trade into the sidelines.

Pirates. The Portuguese still had to eal with problems on their new route. The South China Sea was full of pirates. This was partly because Japanese and Chinese merchants were forbidden to trade with one another. The pirates acted as middlemen, trading with both sides.

The Portuguese finally put the pirates down. For this they were rewarded by the Chinese. When they were still new to the Spice Route, the Portuguese had been thrown out of Canton when one of their captains had behaved very badly there. Even after they put down the pirates, they were not allowed to return to Canton. But they were allowed to settle on the peninsula of Macao, downriver from Canton, in 1557.

Meanwhile, Portuguese merchants were also trading with Japan. So they gradually took over the pirates' role. They became the middlemen between these two great Eastern nations. We can appreciate how important the Portuguese had become when we take account of the fact that Portuguese was the main language spoken to do business all along the Spice Route at that time.

Traders from this 16th-century Portuguese ship have set up an makeshift market on the Japanese shore. (Museu de Arte Antiga, Lisbon)

THE SPANISH ON THE SPICE ROUTE

Magellan and the Spanish Explorations. The Portuguese were not the only Europeans in the region. In 1552, Ferdinand Magellan sailed across the Pacific Ocean to the Philippine Islands. Although Magellan was Portuguese, he was sponsored by the King of Spain.

Magellan's voyage helped to prove that the world was round. He also gave the Spanish their first foothold in the East. Although the Philippines had a culture and political system of its own, Magellan claimed this land for Spain. As with Portugal, Spain's military power made this claim a reality.

The Spanish in Manila. The Spanish failed to establish themselves in the Spice Islands. But they did found a major port at Manila, which is now the capital of the modern-day Philippines.

The Spanish had already claimed much land in Mexico. Now each year they sent galleons—big ships—between Manila and Acapulco in Mexico. These ships brought Mexican silver to the Spice route, which was welcomed throughout the East.

The Spanish in Japan. The Spanish tried to find a friendly port in Japan, as well; they had claimed land in California, and they wanted a resting port on the way back there from the Spice Route. For a time, it looked as though Japan might welcome the Spanish. They even sent ships across the Pacific to Acapulco from Japan in 1613 and 1616. But the Japanese became insulted by the Spanish missionaries, who tried to convert the Japanese from their own religions to Christianity. Eventually, the Japanese refused entry to the Spanish.

COMPETITION FROM OTHER POWERS

The Chinese. Other great nations remained powerful on the Spice Route. Toward the end of the 16th century, China's Ming Dynasty revived its naval forces. Then Chinese ships carried large numbers of immigrants throughout Southeast Asia, especially to Indonesia, Malaya, and the Philippines.

The Chinese immigrants set up their own communities in these new lands. They often continued to trade with their home country, preserved their own langugage and traditions, and considered themselves Chinese rather than members of their new countries.

These immigrants also traded with the Portuguese, the Spanish, and with other Asians.

The Dutch. The Dutch first established a foothold on the Spice Route in 1596, at Bantam, on the island of Java (in modern Indonesia), and soon the Dutch East India Company began trading in the Molucca Islands. The Dutch only had sailing experience in the cold waters of the North Atlantic, and therefore, they depended on the Portuguese for knowledge of the Spice Route.

They had the help of the Jewish merchants, who had been expelled from Portugal around the same time that Jews had been expelled from Spain. The Dutch welcomed these people, who settled in Amsterdam. These Jewish immigrants had both practical experience in Asian trading and money to finance overseas trade.

The British. Like the Dutch, the British only had sailing experience in the North Atlantic, and they had relied on Portuguese information about the geography of the East. But they were stronger than the Portuguese, and were determined to enter the profitable Spice Route trade.

Just as the Portuguese had won the Spice Route by force, so did they lose it by force. The Dutch and the British even joined forces for a time, against the Portuguese.

Decline of the Portuguese. The Portuguese had been strong enough to take the Spice Route away from the Moslems. But they were unable to keep out other Europeans.

Portugal was only a small country, with a small population; it could not even handle the Spice Route trade by itself. It had to rely on local people to collect products, which they sent around the Cape of Good Hope to the Portuguese.

As you can see, the Portuguese were stretched too thin in the Far East. They resisted the other Europeans as best they could. But the first half of the 17th century saw a long slow decline in Portuguese power. In 1612, the Portuguese lost a key battle to a smaller British fleet. In 1622, they lost the major port of Ormuz (today's Hormuz). Between 1638 and 1640, all Portuguese traders were expelled from Japan. In 1641, they gave up Malacca to the Dutch.

Though they lost many other Spice Route colonies, the Portuguese remained secure in Goa, on the southwestern coast of India. (From Linschoten, *Itinerario*, Amsterdam, 1595–6, British Museum)

The clove trade of Amboina (Ambon) Island would later be the object of fierce competition between the Dutch and British. (Nederlandsch Historisch Scheepvaart Museum, Amsterdam)

Over the next 20 years, the Portuguese lost almost all of their Spice Route ports. They kept only Goa, Macao, Mombasa (in modern Kenya), and Mozambique. These remained Portuguese colonial areas for several more centuries. Mozambique remained part of Portuguese East Africa until 1975.

THE AGE OF PIRATES

Many Powers in the East. Although the Dutch and the British drove out the Portuguese to some extent, neither of them took control of the Spice Route as the Portuguese had. Nor did any other power.

The Dutch were the strongest power in the region, especially in the East Indies. But the British and the newly arrived French tried to gain strength in India. Meanwhile, the Moslems kept control of the Arabian region and gradually regained power in East Africa.

With so many different powers competing for control, political alliances on the Spice Route continued to shift. Europeans attacked each other as well as Moslems and other Easterners, each trying to gain a bigger portion of the profitable trade.

Pirates of Many Lands. All of the competing powers were fair game for the pirates who once again sprang up along the route. Japanese pirates operated in the China Sea, and Malay pirates were strong in the East Indies, where they attacked both Spice Route traders and the Spanish galleons trading out of Manila.

In the Bay of Bengal, two groups of pirates worked among the islands, especially off Chittagong. The *Muggs* were mostly local people. The *Feringhis*, on the other hand, were people of mostly Portuguese or other European descent. A special navy had to be formed just to fight them.

There were also a few British pirates in the Bay of Bengal. Along with the other two groups, they were partly controlled by the end of the 17th century.

Hindu Pirates. In the islands off India's Malabar Coast, a group called the Marathas set up a pirate empire. These people practiced the religion of *Hinduism*.

The Hindu Marathas had been discriminated against by the ruling Moslem Mughals and became very strong pirates who could not be subdued until the mid-1700's, when the British East India Company's Bombay Marine became strong enough to overcome them.

The Coast of Pirates. Farther west were the Omanis. They were Moslems, holding the horn of the Arabian Peninsula. This region, at the south of the Persian Gulf, was so dominated by pirates that it was called the Coast of Pirates.

The Omanis built their navy using what they had learned from the Portuguese. They took the main islands of the Persian Gulf, except Ormuz, and threatened Goa and Diu. As they grew stronger, they became a nation.

Then the nation of Oman attacked the Portuguese territories in Arabia and in East Africa. First they took Muscat, which today is the capital city of Oman. Then they took Mombasa, capital of today's Kenya. They moved on down the coast to Pemba and Zanzibar, though the Portuguese stopped them in Mozambique.

A new Persian fleet joined with the Portuguese in the 1700s. They slowed the Omanis somewhat. Portugal was able to take back Mombasa in 1728.

The Omani sailors were strong enough to threaten Europeans into the 1800s, until the Bombay marine cleared them out of the Persian Gulf. Nevertheless, they kept much of East Africa. They and other Moslem peoples kept the Europeans from dominating the Red Sea region.

THE FIGHT FOR CONTROL

Though the risks were great, the possible riches of the Spice Route attracted traders to its many ports. Different powers tried to control activity on the route, or to protect their own countries from other nations.

Japan. The Japanese, for example, deeply resented attempts by Catholic missionaries to convert them from their own religions. They saw this as disrespectful. They also thought that if many of their people followed a European religion, that would give the Europeans more power over them.

Therefore, in 1640, the Japanese threw the Catholics out of Japan. Many of the Japanese who had converted to Catholicism were murdered. The Dutch were allowed to stay in Japan. Their religion was Protestant—a form of Christianity different from Catholicism. The Dutch Protestants had not tried to convert the Japanese. Therefore, they were allowed to stay. But even they were kept apart from the Japanese. They were restricted to a human-made island called Deshima in the port of Hirado for over two centuries.

The Dutch were allowed to stay partly because of a British pilot named William Adams. Adams was shipwrecked on a Dutch vessel in the early 1600s. He became an advisor to the shogun, the Japanese military ruler. As an advisor, he was able to influence the Japanese to favor northern European Protestants.

Japan withdrew from the rest of the world. The Japanese realized that the Europeans had superior military power. They were concerned that interacting with the Europeans would lead to Europe dominating them.

The Dutch. Although they were not always successful, the Dutch set up some rules of their own. They tried to control the pepper market, but they failed. They did control the pepper in parts of Indonesia, but some of the best pepper came from India's Malabar Coast, where other Europeans operated.

However, the Dutch did maintain a monopoly on cloves and nutmeg. They set aside particular areas as "spice farms." Then they destroyed clove and nutmeg trees elsewhere in Indonesia. They wrecked the local economy—but they made sure that they completely controlled the growing and selling of these particular spices.

The Dutch could be ruthless about protecting their monopoly. In 1722 a Dutch governor beheaded 26 employees in one day, just for smuggling the precious spices. According to one anonymous writer "No lover ever guarded his beloved more jealously than did the Dutch the Island of Amboina where the clover trees grow."

However, the Dutch monopoly did not last forever. By the early 18th century, French colonists were able to get hold of some of the precious plants. The French took them to the western parts of the Indian Ocean, particularly to Zanzibar and Pemba. These places soon became a second major source of spices.

The Dutch and the Chinese. The Dutch also tried to force the Chinese out of trade on the Spice Route. Once again, they were prepared to be ruthless. In 1623, Jan Coen, governor of the Dutch East India Company, wrote to his directors about what it would take to get rid of the Chinese completely:

> …the Chinese say that…if we want to keep them from [Manila], we will have to imprison or kill all the people we get hold of in order to make the fear of losing life and property greater…than the hope of making profit[.] [F]or as long as the poor are not in bodily danger, the rich will always venture the goods [for poor people to sell]…

China. Meanwhile, the Chinese had set rules and limits of their own. In China itself, European traders were limited to two ports—Macao and its up-river neighbor, Canton (Guangzhou). Like the Japanese, the Chinese resented the Catholics who tried to convert them. They feared that the Europeans wanted to use both religion and military power to dominate them.

Therefore, even the foreigners who were in Macao and Canton were restricted. They could deal only with Chinese merchant associations called *hongs*, and they could live and work only in restricted foreign quarters.

At first, the Chinese were not very interested in foreign goods. After all, they could manufacture their own fine silks and porcelains, and they could trade for spices with the Indians and with their own Southeast Asian Chinese colonies.

Therefore, the Chinese were for a while interested only in the Spanish silver dollars that were brought into the region by galleons from Manila. These silver dollars became the standard money of the region from the late 1500s through the 1700s.

Traders later found other goods of interest to the Chinese. American traders came to China from either the Cape of Good Hope or Cape Horn, at the tip of South America. They brought a highly prized herb called ginseng, which grows in eastern North America. They also brought some unusual goods from the Pacific, such as furs and birds' nests. British traders also brought these goods to China.

After the arrival of Europeans, Canton, shown here in the early 18th century, once again became the main Chinese port. (British Museum)

THE AGE OF RIVALRY

The late 18th and early 19th century saw increasing rivalry among Europeans on the Spice Route.

The Dutch Lose Power. The Dutch continued to operate along the eastern end of the Spice Route. But by now, they had lost much of their earlier strength. They kept their trading monopoly with the Japanese—although a few Chinese merchants also managed to do some business with Japan. However, this once-strong nation was no longer a major world power.

The British-French Struggle. Instead, the major battle on the Spice Route was between the British and the French, each of whom wanted to control the Indian Ocean. This fight was part of a much larger British-French struggle.

Between 1740 and 1815, the British and the French were involved in a worldwide series of wars. Along with various German states, they were rapidly becoming the dominant powers in Europe as well as the dominant colonial powers worldwide. That is, they now controlled much of the territory of Africa, Asia, and the Americas, as well as much of their trade.

The French Revolution and Napoleon. In 1789, the French Revolution occurred, overthrowing the system of monarchy and setting up a republic of the people. This radical action led to a series of wars. There were civil wars inside the country, as the nobility fought to hold the land that the people wanted to take from them. There were also wars between France and its neighbors.

Out of the French Revolution came a soldier named Napoleon Bonaparte, who quickly rose to power in the confused time after the Revolution. At first, it seemed that Napoleon wanted to support the French Republic. But eventually, it became clear that he had plans to become a dictator. He also wanted to conquer all of Europe, as the Romans had done during their centuries of imperial power. He named himself emperor and took control of much of Europe.

Napoleon and the Spice Route. When Napoleon came to power, the French had bases on the Spice Route. Sometimes they had allied themselves with the Dutch to protect their holdings. Nevertheless, both countries had gradually been losing ground to the British. Had it not been for the might of Napoleon, they might have been pushed out of the Indian Ocean altogether.

But Napoleon Bonaparte invaded Egypt. Thus he put pressure on the British from the Red Sea. The British had to send ships to the Middle East, which meant they had fewer ships with which to fight the French and Dutch elsewhere on the Spice Route.

Napoleon and the Suez Canal. Napoleon had many visionary ideas. He had an engineer explore the idea of a canal at Suez, linking the Red Sea with the Mediterranean. Such a canal would cut down travel time between Europe and the eastern Spice Route. Trade could still be conducted entirely by sea, but would not have to go all the way around Africa.

Napoleon's Suez Canal was never built. However, this idea—which the Egyptians had also had many centuries B.C.—would eventually come to fruition. After a great deal of success in many parts of Europe in military engagements, Napoleon was finally defeated in 1815 by the British and Prussians at the Battle of Waterloo. This loss marked the end of his empire.

British Power on the Spice Route. With Napoleon defeated, the British were clearly the major power on the Spice Route. They had almost total control of India and Ceylon. They did, however, return Java and Malacca to the Dutch, who maintained control of what is now Indonesia until the long war for independence in 1945-1949.

The British set up their own key port in the East Indies, though, at the island of Singapore, off the tip of Malaya. This British outpost, founded in 1819, became the main trading port on the Spice Route.

There had not been one dominant power on the Spice Route since Portuguese power declined. The Portuguese language had been used on the Spice Route into the 1800s; each ship carried Portuguese interpreters, and ports were well stocked with Portuguese dictionaries for traders' use. Now the main language on the route became English. This process was accelerated with the entry of English-speaking traders from the United States.

The standard currency also changed. For centuries, it had been Spanish silver dollars, generally brought from Mexico in Manila bound galleons, or at least made from Mexican silver. With the rise of the British and the end of the galleon runs, the standard coin along the Spice Route became the Indian rupee, from the Eastern country which Britain had under its control.

THE OPIUM WARS

The British had wanted to trade with the Chinese. But the Chinese saw no reason to trade their fine goods for inferior European ones. Because the Chinese controlled foreign trade so completely, restricting it to Canton, it was difficult for the British to expand their trade.

Opium: A Dangerous Drug. Then the British East India Company found a commodity that interested at least some Chinese—opium. Opium is a drug related to the modern drug of heroin. People who smoke opium regularly quickly become addicted to it. Serious opium addicts lose interest in doing anything but smoking and dreaming their opium dreams. Therefore, the Chinese had made opium illegal.

Opium, however, was grown in India, which the British effectively controlled. The East India Company secretly supplied opium to some traders, who secretly exchanged it for silks and tea. The British grew to love tea, which became their national drink. But the tea was gained at the price of much suffering in China, caused by the importing of opium.

British Opium Trade Grows. The British did not trade opium directly; they used middlemen. With the much-desired drug opening doors for them, these small traders made their way through many rivers and harbors along China's unpatrolled coastline. Gradually, they established contacts outside Canton.

In the late 1700s and early 1800s, the East India Company became very eager to supply opium to the Chinese, because of the tremendous profits it was making.

In its eagerness, the company employed outside captains. These traders became big-time smugglers. They used fast clipper ships, of a type first built in Baltimore. The traders even had a yearly race to be the first to bring each crop of opium into China.

Legal European merchants were still restricted to the *hongs*, the official merchants' associations in Canton. But private merchants and smugglers worked out of Lintin Island, in Canton Bay, penetrating the poorly patrolled Chinese river and seacoast.

By the turn of the 19th century, these traders were bringing about 4,500 chests of opium into China each year. Some 30 years later, by the late 1830s, the amount had grown to almost 10 times that. The Chinese laws against opium had little effect.

The First Opium War. In 1838, the Chinese did more than pass laws. They seized British goods and cut off food and water to any British traders. This forced the British to withdraw to Macao and then to Hong Kong.

For a little while, the British continued to trade through traders from the United States. Then they attacked the Chinese. They blockaded the Yangtze River and took positions along the coast up to the city of Shanghai.

The British won easily; the first Opium War, as it was called, ended in 1842. Britain took advantage of its victory to seize even more from the Chinese. They took Hong Kong island (which is still a British territory), as well as trading rights in Canton (Guangzhou), Shanghai, and several other cities.

The United States and France quickly acquired the same trading rights. China, the country that had been so eager to protect itself from foreigners, was now at their mercy.

Ironically, the same opium trade that had enriched the British East India Company for years now led to problems for the company. Until the end of the first Opium War, the East India Company had had a monopoly on trade with China. Now two other Western powers were involved, and others were soon to follow.

The Second Opium War. Chinese junks had been trading on the Spice Route over the centuries of European control. Now, as a result of China's defeat in the First Opium War, they were forced out of the long-distance part of the trade. The Europeans wanted this profitable enterprise for themselves, and they had the military power to take it.

The Chinese did continue to work with European traders in ports like Hong Kong and Shanghai. These quickly became the most "Europeanized" of China's cities. Shanghai, a fine deep-water port at the mouth of the Yangtze River, soon grew larger than Canton.

By the 1850s, the Europeans wanted still more, which China did not want to give. The British and the French attacked again—though their attack was delayed when the British had to withdraw some troops in 1857 to deal with a mutiny in India.

By 1858, however, the Europeans occupied Canton. They used this power base to force China to open many more ports, including Taipei, on the island of Formosa, present-day Taiwan.

But the Europeans were still not satisfied. When the Chinese resisted, they attacked inland and looted Beijing, the capital of China. They destroyed the famous Summer Palace, making it quite clear to the Chinese that they were ready to do anything in order to expand their trade.

The Chinese gave in. At the end of this second Opium War, trading in opium was legalized. The British demanded further payment, including the peninsula of Kowloon, which was added to the colony of Hong Kong.

This Chinese ship, anchored along the coast, dwarfs the rowboats that bring traders to its side. (New York Public Library)

THE OPENING OF JAPAN

Other major changes were taking place along the eastern end of the Spice Route. Japan was still closed to all Europeans except the Dutch. But Japan had been observing what was happening to China. The Japanese understood that the powers that had attacked China would soon begin to attack them.

Therefore, they had begun to learn about European culture in order to compete with the Europeans. Dutch knowledge in such areas as astronomy, geography, and medicine was highly regarded. The Japanese began to develop their army, metal industry, and shipyards.

Perry "Opens" Japan. Thus, when U.S. Commodore Matthew Perry anchored his warships in Tokyo Bay in 1853, the Japanese were to some extent prepared. Perry went to Japan with the purpose of opening trade between that country and the United States. He brought warships with him to back up his diplomacy with military power. The Japanese were not totally surprised—but neither were they prepared to resist.

The Japanese negotiated with Perry, agreeing to open the ports of Shimoda and Hakodate to America. However, these ports were not open for trading, only for repair and resupply of ships that were making the long return trip from the Spice Route back across the Pacific. (This was the concession Spain had wanted in the previous century, when its galleons were still crossing the ocean between Mexico and Manila.) This agreement resulted in what is known as the "opening of Japan."

Within five years, though, the Japanese were forced to open these and the additional ports of Kanagawa and Nagasaki to European traders. Within 10 years, several other ports were also opened for trading. Meanwhile, Western merchants had developed the fishing village of Yokohama as a major port.

Russia Enters the Far East. In the mid-19th century, Russia held a huge empire stretching from Europe through Asia. It was a relatively primitive country, whose people still lived under a *feudal* system: until 1861, most Russians were *serfs*, peasants who were required by law to live and work on the land of their masters with hardly more civil rights than slaves.

Despite these backward conditions, Russia was a powerful nation and a rapidly expanding empire. It expanded into the lands of many different peoples, including those living to the east in Siberia and the Middle East.

When they had expanded eastward all the way to the Pacific, the Russians established a main port at Vladivostok, just north of Korea. Naturally, they wanted to trade with Japan, but the Japanese refused. Thereupon the Russians attacked the Japanese settlement on the island of Sakhalin, which both Russia and Japan claimed as their own.

The Japanese were not fond of the Russians. But when they were forced to trade with other Europeans, they began to trade with Russia as well. Likewise, China expanded trade with Russia as it was forced to do with the other powers of Europe.

The Suez Canal

As we have seen, by the first few decades of the 19th century, the Europeans controlled almost all of the Spice Route. Their coming changed the whole way business was done.

Up until the Europeans had invaded the area, the Spice Route had been a local route. During the period of European control, traders gathered goods from the area immediately around them, and stored these goods in whichever major port was nearby. Then a ship equipped for long-distance trade would pick up goods along the Spice Route, stopping at several major ports along the way. The ship would carry the goods from East to West via another route, called the Cape of Good Hope Route (see Chapter 4). Obviously the voyage was very long.

But by the mid-19th century, with the Spice Route completely under their control and peace established in Europe, Europeans began to look at how they could get Spice Route goods back to their lands more easily.

The logical place to look was at the western end of the Spice Route—the Middle East. Moslem control in the area was weak.

Before the opening of the Suez Canal, travelers tried to shorten the route to the East by crossing the shifting sands of the Suez Isthmus. (*Illustrated London News*, April 25, 1857)

Perhaps, thought the Europeans, they could take advantage of this. The idea of a canal at Suez was born again.

Negotiating for the Suez Canal. As we saw, the ancient Egyptians had once built their own "Suez Canal" (see Chapter 1). The new canal involved the Egyptians once again.

A French citizen, Ferdinand de Lesseps, had a friendship with an Egyptian viceroy. At the time, the Egyptians were under the control of the Turks, who had appointed the viceroy to rule for them in Egypt. This viceroy, however, was probably more influenced by the French and the English than he was by the Turks. He warmly welcomed the idea of a canal and gave de Lesseps the right to build it.

Then came a harder step—getting the Europeans to concur. At this time, the British controlled the lion's share of the Spice Route. They also held a monopoly on the Cape of Good Hope Route—the route from Asia to Europe that went around the southern tip of Africa. They feared that the opening of a new route would deprive this monopoly of its value.

The British fears were well founded, as this is precisely what the French intended. Even though the end of the Napoleonic Wars had brought peace between Britain and France, the two countries were still bitter rivals. And even Napoleon had said that "in order to destroy England it is necessary for us to possess Egypt."

Nevertheless, de Lesseps finally gained approval from Britain and France to build the canal, as well as money from both countries. He began digging the canal in the spring of 1859.

Building the Suez Canal. Imagine the difficulty of cutting out huge portions of earth to make a passageway wide enough for a steamship! The construction of this engineering feat took 10 long years.

At first the backbreaking work was done by slave laborers. Some 60,000 so-called "forced" laborers did the digging and hauling of dirt. Protests at the time led the engineers to replace some of the workers with machines—but many other slaves continued to work on the canal.

When the Suez Canal was built, it stretched 100 miles, from the port of Suez, through several lakes, to the new city of Ismailia. Then the canal ran out to the new settlement of Port Said on the Mediterranean Sea.

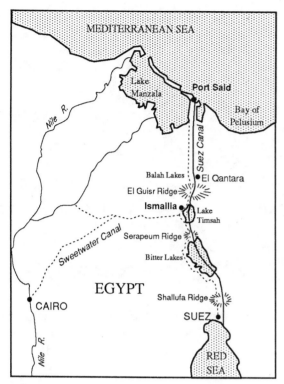

The Suez Canal

Some canals use many *locks*. Locks are necessary on canal routes where the water level varies. A lock consists of two gates which let water in or out to raise or lower boats from one level to another. The Panama Canal, connecting the Atlantic and Pacific oceans has many locks. The Suez Canal, however, did not need locks. At its narrowest, the Suez is only 150 feet wide. At other places, however, it is so wide that ships can easily pass each other.

Opening the Canal. The opening of the Suez was a grand occasion. The ceremony featured two groups of ships. An Egyptian group set off from the Red Sea, while an international group set off from the Mediterranean Sea. Each group sailed into the canal, to meet at the central port of Ismailia. The two seas were finally officially connected.

Many European kings and queens attended this opening ceremony. Thousands of visitors came to witness the historic event. The Europeans were proud and excited. The French Empress

Eugenie even cried with pride. Perhaps the Africans, Asians and Middle Easterners had somewhat different feelings, for the canal signaled another increase of European power over their lands.

EUROPEAN CONQUEST

Now that the Suez Canal was open, the Cape of Good Hope Route fell into disuse. Sailing ships also fell into disuse. Ill winds and hidden reefs made the Red Sea a bad place for the great clippers and East India ships. These ships also had to be towed through the canal, since no winds could blow them through. This towing was expensive and raised the cost of the journey.

Steamships, on the other hand, were logical transport for canal travel. They burned coal to produce steam, which drove their engines without the need for wind. Sailing ships were better for the little travel that still took place on the Cape of Good Hope Route, since this long route required too much coal for steamships to carry easily.

Colonization Along the Spice Route. Now that it was so much easier to get from Europe to the East, far more Europeans traveled and settled along the Spice Route. Before the Suez Canal had opened, Europeans could reach the Indian Ocean only by undertaking a hard journey of many months. Because women were then considered unable to undergo hardships, most of these travelers were men, many of whom married local women in India.

The Portuguese, in particular, had sent only men out into the Spice Route. When the Dutch were in power there, they had tried to recreate their way of life in the East Indies. But women of the time were not allowed to be sailors or traders. They went overseas as wives and daughters only—and many of these were killed in shipwrecks or robbed by pirates. The Dutch government decided instead to keep women at home and have men marry the local women of the East Indies.

The English and French set up a pattern called *nabobism*, which enabled *nabobs* to bring their families from Europe. Earlier Europeans had been traders, whose requests were granted by the rulers of the countries they visited. But the French and the British were actually becoming imperial rulers, annexing the countries they visited in a way that earlier traders had not been able to.

Because they were extending the reaches of their empires, these Europeans set themselves up as *nabobs*, or princes. (The word nabob comes from the Indian word *nawab*, or Mughal prince.) These eastern lands became *colonies*—territories under outside political control.

The British settled in solidly in India, building settlements like Fort St. George, at Madras, on the Coromandel Coast. (British Museum)

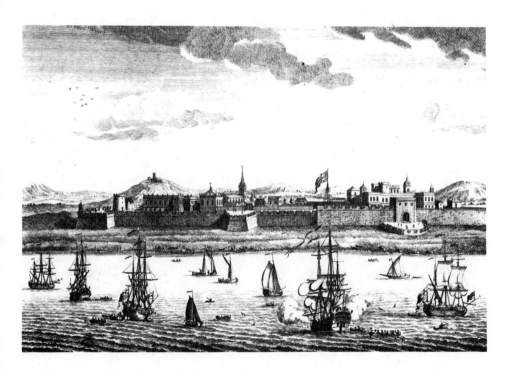

With this new control, plus the new, easier steamship travel, these nabobs were able to bring their wives and families from Europe. Thus European traders and businessmen also carried on their way of life, separate from the native peoples of India and other Eastern lands they inhabited.

This process had begun even before the Suez Canal was opened. The canal, however, gave a great boost to the trend, and Europeans expanded their colonies into Africa and the East.

The Europeans Colonize Africa.
East Africa felt the effects of this increased European presence even more sharply than other regions. Previously, Europeans had not focused their interest on East Africa. They had been happy to let Moslems keep control of it, using it only as a series of trading ports from which they could pick up precious Eastern goods.

For their part, the Moslems had remained on their coastal strip, making only a few trading trips inland, to the countries where native Africans ruled. Slave trade on this coast had been controlled by the Sultan of Muscat (in the present country of Oman), once he had defeated the Portuguese in 1698. In 1841, the sultanate expanded its control slightly by establishing a new empire centered on the island of Zanzibar.

The British had once profited from their slave trade with the Moslems. Then they outlawed it for all British citizens in the early 1800s. Although slavery continued in the United States and other

Spices gradually replaced slaves as the main "products" handled in Zanzibar's markets. (*Graphic*, 1873)

parts of the world, the slave trade was no longer the huge, profitable enterprise it had once been for Europeans and Americans.

Nevertheless, the British were still interested in East Africa for other reasons, and this interest grew after the opening of the Suez Canal. Explorers, missionaries, traders, and settlers began to probe the inner lands of East Africa. They went into the heartland of the area, past the thin coastal strip under Moslem control. They began to establish British control over huge sections of Africa.

Not only the British were interested in acquiring pieces of Africa. The French annexed Djibouti (which they called French Somaliland) on the East African coast. The Italians moved in farther down the Somali coast, while the Germans moved through Zanzibar to Tanganyika and Kenya.

The British Colonize Africa.
The Suez Canal made Africa more attractive to Europeans, because the region was now easier to reach. The British in particular were interested in Africa, for many reasons.

The Suez Canal had levied high charges against all ships that passed through it. Nevertheless, it had not been a financial success for Egypt because it cost so much to maintain. Almost half of the shares of the Suez Canal Company, including those of the Egyptian viceroy, went on sale. They were bought up by the British government under Prime Minister Benjamin Disraeli. Suddenly, the Suez Canal was no longer controlled by a private company whose investors were private citizens. Instead, the Canal came under the control of the British government.

With their new control of the Suez Canal, the British virtually controlled European access to East Africa. This was a powerful incentive for them to expand their own control of that region.

Britain also expanded its holdings in the Middle East. While they were under control of the Turkish government, the Egyptians resented foreigners, both the Turks who ruled them and the British who had come to hold so much power over them. In the 1880s, the Egyptians rioted against the British, who then stepped in to assume control of that country.

From Egypt, the British moved to take the Sudan, Somaliland, and Kenya. The British controlled so much land in so many places around the world that they coined the phrase "The sun never sets on the British Empire." That meant that the British ruled so many lands in the East and West that even when the sun set in one part of their empire, it shone in another.

Industrialization. Besides colonization another important social change of the time was *industrialization*, the growth of industry. New tools and industries were giving northern Europeans skills that they had never had before. In the early centuries of their control of the Spice Route, they had used their military power to gain access to and buy the beautiful goods of the East. Now industralization meant that Europeans could use machines to produce high-quality cloth and tableware in their own countries.

Skilled workers in India, China, and other Eastern lands had become dependent on selling goods to Europe. Now they were largely thrown out of work. Weavers and metalworkers in northern Europe were taking their place. The British in particular moved rapidly to build factories and find British workers to fill them. Often, this was done through harsh laws that forced workers to take the first available job.

Mines and Plantations. If the Europeans were not interested in Eastern-manufactured goods, they were still interested in Eastern raw materials. Europeans began to develop coffee, tea, and rubber *plantations*—huge farms run by Europeans and worked by local laborers. Often these laborers had been peasants with land of their own that was taken by the Europeans. They were then forced to work for the Europeans under difficult and impoverished conditions. Some said the plantation workers were not much better than slaves.

In addition to local laborers, poorly paid and overworked laborers from India and China moved throughout the Indian Ocean area to fill the Europeans' enormous need for workers. These Indian and Chinese workers were called *coolies*. Because they were part of the process of the European takeover, which frequently destroyed the local economy, these coolies were resented by the local workers, even hated. They were willing to work for low wages, so they were further disliked by local people, who then had to take the same low wages. Often, this resentment took the form of ethnic hatred, and sometimes violence broke out.

Colonialism Continues. These immigrants were not limited to supplying plantation labor. They also worked as crews on trading ships—under European officers, of course. And the Europeans used these ships to continue their takeover of the East.

Most of the world was carved up by the countries of Europe and the United States. The Netherlands took Indonesia; the British added Burma, Malaya, and part of Borneo to their previous holdings of India and Ceylon; France took Indochina; the United States took the Philippines from Spain after the Spanish-American War.

The Japanese also wanted to colonize areas they could. Their navy had only been modernized in the final decades of the 19th century. Nevertheless, the Japanese were strong enough to break China's hold on the island of Taiwan and the peninsula of Liaodong. By 1905 Japan had taken Korea. Also in 1905, the Japanese defeated the Russian Empire, which had controlled parts of Manchuria, in China, and southern Sakhalin Island, near Japan. Now the Japanese were a colonial power.

World War I

By 1914, most of the rest of the world had been carved up by European countries, Japan, and the United States. Europe, in particular, had become involved in a dangerous system of international competition, as countries fought over new colonies and territories. At the same time, the European nations had made many *alliances*—agreements between nations pledged to help each other in battle if one were attacked.

Thus the situation in Europe was extremely volatile. If any one national was attacked, it could call to its aid another nation with whom it had an alliance. That nation could in turn call on its allies, and so on. Likewise, the attacker nation could call on *its* allies—and all Europe could become embroiled in war.

This is exactly what happened. The situation was further complicated by the fact that so many European powers were empires made up of many differnt lands and peoples. The European empires controlled colonies in Asia, Africa, and the Middle East, as we have seen. They also controlled subject peoples in Europe. For example, the Austro-Hungarian Empire controlled the many different peoples of the Balkans, as well as much of eastern Europe. The Russian Empire also controlled many peoples in eastern Europe.

Therefore, when war finally broke out, it involved almost the entire world—hence the name, *World War*. When the war was over, the map of Europe was redrawn. Peoples who had been part of huge empires suddenly took political control of their own lands; the old empires had broken up.

However, the new era of *self-determination*, or freedom from foreign political control, applied only to Europe. The countries along the Spice Route were for the most part still colonies. The empires that ruled these colonies were weakened, but they still exercised authority.

The British and Oil in the Middle East. The war had little direct effect on the Spice Route. However, there were some shifts in political control. The most notable was the replacement of the Turks by the still-powerful British as the dominant power in the Middle East. The British soon discovered and started to exploit the resource for which the region is now best known: oil.

Oil had begun to become an important resource even before World War I. In fact, much oil had traveled through the Suez Canal from oil-rich Russia to the Far East. But in 1917, the Russians revolted against the tsar, or emperor. World War I was still going on, and the tsar's government was very much weakened by the conflict. The new revolutionary government was not able to continue old levels of oil production. It was also being attacked by various European nations which did not like the new system of government brought

about by the Revolution. As a result Europe could not get oil from Russia any longer.

Thus, when the British discovered oil in the Middle East, they found a source of this important fuel that was to remain important into our own day. The Spice Route had now become an important oil route.

Colonialism and Resistance. Meanwhile, proud Eastern peoples were fighting hard to throw off European control of their countries. With the weakening of the European empires after World War I, the balance of world power was beginning to shift.

Soon there was a republic in China, inspired in large part by Chinese resentment of the foreigners who had forced them to trade under unequal conditions for so many years. Residents of India were also organizing a freedom movement against British control. So were people in many other nations. Many of these would eventually win their independence after Europeans were weakened further by World War II.

Foreign control was far from dead, however. Indeed, the European nations were still trying to win more colonies.

Pilgrims bound for Mecca who arrived by sea were brought into Jiddah's harbor by these small sailing dhows. (From Richard H. Sanger, *The Arabian Peninsula*, Cornell University Press)

The period after World War I was a period of instability in Europe. World War I had set the British, the French, and later, the Italians and the Americans against the Germans, the Austro-Hungarian Empire and the Turkish Ottoman Empire. When the Germans, Austrians and Turks lost, the victorious nations demanded that they pay huge sums of money in damages. Germany, already weakened by the war, was further weakened by the huge sums that France, especially, demanded.

Germany found it impossible to regain its economic health. Many people were very poor. Prices went up faster than most people could afford. In this atmosphere of disatisfaction, people looked desperately for a solution—any solution—to their problems. Adolf Hitler, a political leader, helped develop the system of *fascism*, in which the government takes almost total control of every aspect of life, allowing a small, powerful group to rule.

Even though Italy had been on the "winning" side of World War I, it, too, was a poor country, one that had never fully developed its industry or modernized to the extent that the northern European countries had. Fascism rose in Italy, too.

In both Germany and Italy, the idea of fascism was bound up with the idea of expansion and empire. The Italians moved against Abyssinia—present-day Ethiopia—which they tried to annex as a colony. Eventually, the British drove them out, but their attack started a new period of troubles on the western end of the Spice Route.

Meanwhile, on the eastern end of the route, the Japanese were continuing to expand their colonial holdings. In the 1930s, they invaded and took large parts of China. At the same time, Hitler was expanding Germany's borders in Europe.

WORLD WAR II

With the fascist countries seeking to expand, war was inevitable. Japan, Germany, and Italy formed the *Axis* against Britain and France, who were known as the *Allies*. When Japan attacked the U.S. Navy at Pearl Harbor in 1941, the United States joined the Allies.

Japan and the Eastern Spice Route. Meanwhile, Japan moved to expand its wartime control of Southeast Asia. It took Singapore, Hong Kong, Indochina, Malaya, Burma, Indonesia, and the Philippines. The Japanese navy even raided India and Ceylon and threatened northern Australia.

The Japanese navy did not control the whole of the Spice Route. If they had tried in 1942, they might have succeeded. By mid-1942, however, the Allies revived and defeated the Japanese in the Coral Sea. They had turned the tide of war along the eastern end of the Spice Route.

Germany and the Western Spice Route. Germany was still active in North Africa. The German general known as the Desert Fox, Erwin Rommel, even threatened the Suez Canal. But Germany did not succeed. The westen part of the Spice Route stayed under Allied control until the Germans, Italians, and Japanese were defeated.

MODERN TIMES

Like World War I, the end of World War II brought many economic and social changes to the entire world, including the Spice Route. Again, there was a shift in power as the old colonies of Africa, Asia, and the Middle East began to win their independence.

Airplanes and Oil Fields. With the increase in manufacturing of automobiles and airplanes, much more oil was needed than ever before, to fuel these new gas-engine-run machines. Oil tankers came to be much of the traffic on the Spice Route, and the Middle East became increasingly important.

The Fight for Independence. Of course, with the defeat of Japan, that power no longer controlled huge parts of Asia. This enabled other changes in the region. The Chinese had been having internal struggles over the type of government they wanted ever since they overthrew their empire and founded a republic, before World War I. In 1949, those Chinese who wanted the country to be communist finally succeeded in their revolution. This brought many changes to China, including more isolation from the West.

An old-style Chinese junk and a modern warship share the waters off Hong Kong, which is still a British territory today. (Willie K. Friar, Panama Canal Commission)

Under the leadership of Mohandas Gandhi (called *Mahatma*, an honorary title meaning "great soul"), India finally won its independence from the British in 1947. After four years of fighting, Indonesia finally overthrew the Dutch in 1949 (although parts of these islands remained under Dutch control for almost twenty years more).

Many other African and Asian nations also won their freedom, redrawing the map of lands along the Spice Route. A few old-style colonies did remain for several more decades, including Macao and East Timor. And African countries off the Spice Route, like Angola and Mozambique, did not become independent until the 1970s. However, the tight grip of European political control had been broken.

Of course, European cultural and economic influence continued throughout the world. And in many places, the process of winning independence was long and bitter. In the Spice Route region of Indochina, for example, the French and Japanese were eventually overthrown, but first Europe and then the United States remained very much involved in the area's political affairs, most notably during the Vietnam War.

Fighting over the Suez Canal. The western end of the Spice Route also saw conflicts between Europeans and their former colonies. After World War II, Egypt pushed to control the Suez Canal. Although the Canal ran through Egypt's territory, it was controlled by a private company that was in turn controlled by the British government.

Egypt did not allow any ships from Israel to pass through the Suez Canal. Israel was itself a new country, the former British controlled territory of Palestine. This Middle Eastern country had been settled by many Jews, mostly from Europe, who were resented by other Middle Easterners. As they saw it, the Jewish European settlers had thrown native Palestinian Arabs out of their homeland. The Jews, on the other hand, believed that they had a right to a land of their own, and based their claim on the fact that the land of Israel had once been theirs during biblical times.

In 1956, Egypt took over the Suez Canal in an effort to assert its control over its own territory. British, French, and Israeli forces attacked Egypt to try to regain control of the canal. But pressure from the United Nations—an international association of countries formed after World War II—forced the three attacking nations to withdraw. Egypt was left in control and continued to refuse access to Israeli ships.

In 1967, the Israelis attacked again, moving across the Sinai Desert to take the east bank of the Suez. During the fighting, ships were sunk in the channel—which, of course, closed the canal.

For eight years, the Suez Canal remained closed. Ships had to use the long Cape of Good Hope Route once again. Finally, in 1979, the first Israeli ship passed through the Suez Canal.

Ironically, during the years that the canal had been closed, new supertankers had been built that were too big to fit in the canal. These now move from the oil-rich countries of the Middle East all the way around Africa. The old Cape of Good Hope Route was put to new use.

The End of the Spice Route. Little remains of the ancient trade conducted along the Spice Route. In our time, there are new products in demand and new means of transport. No longer is it necessary to send sailing ships on long and dangerous journeys to bring back small quantities of precious spices. No longer does Euorpe depend on the fine silk weavers of China for its high-quality cloth. The fabled Spice Route now belongs to history.

Coupland, R. *East Africa and Its Invaders: From the Earliest Times to the Death of Seyyid Said in 1856* (Oxford: Clarendon Press, 1938).

Hoskins, Halford Lancaster. *British Routes to India* (New York: Octagon, 1966; reprint of 1928 edition).

Howe, Sonia E. *In Quest of Spices* (London: Herbert Jenkins, Ltd., 1939).

Miller, J. Innes. *The Spice Trade of the Roman Empire, 29 B.C. to A.D. 641* (Oxford: Clarendon Press, 1969).

Mirsky, Jeannette. *The Great Chinese Travelers* (New York: Pantheon, 1964).

Simkin, C.G.F. *The Traditional Trade of Asia* (London: Oxford University Press, 1968).

Toussaint, Auguste. *History of the Indian Ocean* (Chicago: University of Chicago Press, 1966).

Villiers, Alan. *Monsoon Seas: The Story of the Indian Ocean* (New York: McGraw-Hill, 1952).

Wilson, Arnold T. *The Persian Gulf: An Historical Sketch From the Earliest Times to the Beginning of the Twentieth Century* (London: George Allen & Unwin, 1928).

4

THE CAPE OF GOOD HOPE ROUTE

SAILING AROUND THE TIP OF AFRICA

One of the most important sea routes in human history is the Cape of Good Hope Route. This route linked Europe and Asia for many years. Along with the Spice Route, it was crucial to Europeans who wanted spices, gold, jewels, ceramics, and cloth from the East.

The Cape of Good Hope Route played a major part in the slave trade. This trade caused thousands of African people to be captured and sold into forced labor around the world. They were sold mainly to wealthy landowners in North and South America, where Europeans and their desendants held huge plantations of cotton, coffee, bananas, and other agricultural products.

Finally, the Cape of Good Hope Route was part of Europe's gradual takeover of huge portions of Africa, Asia, and the Middle East. The nations of Europe began annexing these lands from the moment that they first discovered them in the late 15th century. Over the years, the Europeans first took economic then political power. Finally, after World War II, these lands won their independence.

Yet, today, the Cape of Good Hope Route remains important, as super oil tankers carry precious fuel from the Middle East around the tip of Africa up to Europe. Studying the history of this route helps us to understand the long and difficult relationship between Europe and the other continents of the world.

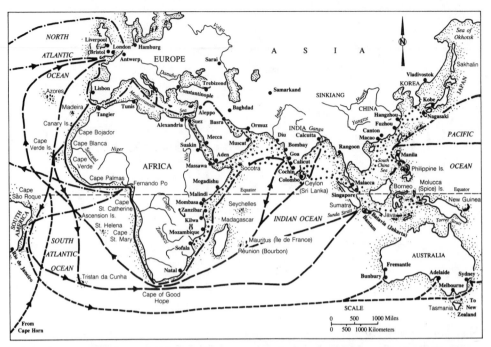

The Cape of Good Hope Route and the Modern Spice Route

— — — Early Cape of Good Hope Route

──────── Main Cape of Good Hope Route

– – – – – – – – Australia Route

· · · · · · · · Spice Route

—·—·— Main Connecting Routes

In Ancient Times

In ancient times, when sailors still used frail boats that depended on winds and currents, parts of the Cape of Good Hope Route were used by Phoenicians, Greeks, and Romans.

The Geography of the Route. Eventually, the route was developed to run south from western Europe, into the Atlantic. It went to the islands off West Africa, including the Canaries and the Cape Verde Islands.

Then the route cut southwest across the Atlantic, almost to the great bulge of South America. After that, it followed the west winds back across the South Atlantic, to the Cape of Good Hope, at the tip of southern Africa.

Why did sailors make this wide swing out into the ocean? For many years, sailors used sailing ships, which depended on winds and currents. In order to make the best use of these natural aids, sailors had to zig-zag across the Atlantic, going miles out of their way but saving time in the end.

The return trip, from Africa back to Europe, was easier, again because of the currents. Going from south to north, ships could stay closer to the African coast. One route followed Africa's east coast, going acrpss the Arabian Sea to India. If sailors took this route, they sometimes stopped at islands like Madagascar, Mauritius, or Réunion.

The other main route cut across the Indian Ocean, heading either for the Bay of Bengal in India or for the rich East Indies, the Spice Islands.

Australia: The Accidental European Discovery. Ships on this route were often blown off course. Interestingly, the continent of Australia was discovered by Europeans in just such ships, many centuries after this route was first used. Australia later became a third main landing place for ships following this route.

East Meets West

After the great days of the Phoenicians, Greeks, and Romans, the West entered a period on decline. Great civilizations flourished in the East, however.

These Eastern civilizations were barely known in Europe. Their goods, however, were well known. Chinese silks, Indian cottons, finely worked gold and silver objects, and precious spices made the long journey from Asia and Africa to Europe.

Even after the fall of the Roman Empire, when Europe itself was little more than a collection of isolated tribal peoples, East-West trade continued. When Europe began to revive, trade with the East increased, too.

The Rise of Islam. Originally, some of the most important traders in Europe were the Italians. The Italian cities of Genoa and Venice rose on East-West trade. Their merchants bought goods in western Asia and shipped them across the Mediterranean for sale in Europe.

Then, in the seventh century, the prophet Elijah Mohammed founded the new religion of Islam. The new religion spread quickly through Africa, Asia, and the Middle East, reaching areas that had once been Christian as well as peoples who had followed other local religions.

The Moslem countries of the Middle East controlled the main sea and land routes from Europe to Asia. They became much less tolerant of the non-Moslems in their midst, particularly the Italian traders who were making such huge profits on the East-West trade. The Moslems fought back by putting tight controls on all goods from the East, and by charging large taxes on them.

The Rise of Spain and Portugal. By the end of the 13th century, Genoa and Venice were not able to continue their trade to the same extent as before. They now had experienced sailors to spare. These skilled men went west, to the ports of Spain and Portugal.

Much of Spain and Portugal had actually been under Moslem rule. These Moslems, often called *Moors*, had a great influence on Spanish culture. Moslem rulers respected both the Christians and the Jews in their territory, and the three religions had for the most part coexisted in peace.

But Christian rulers from northern Spain and Portugal wanted to expel the Moslems. At the same time, they wanted to explore the East further. They were ready to conquer new lands and expand their power.

By the early 14th century, Spanish and Portuguese explorers were using Italian sailors to explore the Atlantic. They went past the Straits of Gibraltar and "rediscovered" the Canary Islands, about 60 miles off the northwest coast of Africa. The Spanish and Portuguese had also "rediscovered" the Azores, islands that were about 800 miles west of Portugal in the uncharted Atlantic.

Of course, the people living on these islands didn't consider these voyages "discoveries"—they had known about their homes all the time! But the Europeans had no idea how big Africa was, or what they might find in the oceans around it. The Cape of Good Hope route had still to be discovered. In fact, the Europeans had not yet even discovered the Cape of Good Hope.

HENRY THE NAVIGATOR

In the early 15th century, a Portuguese prince called Henry the Navigator helped make more discoveries, which would eventually help European sailors realize the size and shape of Africa—and use the Cape of Good Hope Route.

First, Henry set up a base near the town of Sagres, in Portugal. Then he brought together the best talents of his time—experienced ship pilots, mapmakers, astronomers, and mathematicians. Their main task was to find new ways of figuring location and direction in the uncharted waters of the Atlantic.

Many of these experts were Italians experienced in the Mediterranean trade. Others were Jews trained in the fine Moslem centers of learning. They were welcomed by tiny Portugal, whose own population numbered less than 2 million people.

In addition to assembling these people, Henry collected books—sea pilots' logs and chartbooks. He wanted to compile this information so that future navigators would know the safe places to drop anchor, landmarks to get their bearings, and ports where they could get water and food.

However, this Portuguese prince was only interested in helping Portugal. Giving this information to other countries was strictly forbidden. Even two centuries later, there was actually a death penalty for sharing certain maps to India!

The Portuguese in Africa. In 1415, the Portuguese captured Ceuta, a flourishing Moslem trading town on the coast of Morocco. This was turning point for the 21-year-old Prince Henry.

From the prisoners he took, Henry learned about the rich trade routes across the Sahara Desert to Timbuktu, a major commercial and trading center in what is today the country of Mali. Henry was eager to circle around the Arabs who had already set up trading cities on the east coast of Africa. He wanted to find a way to go directly to the African gold.

Henry set out to colonize the islands off the African shore. He planned to use them as stepping stones for exploring the African coast. At first, in 1415, Henry's ships reached as far as Cape Bojador on the west coast of modern-day Morocco (so named by the Portuguese because it was the "Bulging Cape").

This cape—a sandy barrier stretching out into the Atlantic—looks fairly small. To the tiny boats of the time, however, its currents and winds were dangerous. There were also reefs, which could smash a ship or tear a hole in it.

The Portuguese sailors feared Cape Bojador. They thought perhaps the winds would be so strong that once they rounded the cape, they could never return. There were also superstitions about a "Sea of Darkness" that was supposed to lie on the other side.

As sailors were opening up world ocean routes, and discovering a wide variety of new beings in the process, the oceans seemed full of strange monsters. (From Sebastian Munster, *Cosmographia*, 1550, Staatlich Museen zu Berlin)

For 12 years, Henry's explorers went no further than Cape Bojador. They raided Moorish settlements instead of going on. Finally, in 1433, they went further down the coast, past areas under Arab control. This lay the groundwork for the next big step in the history of the Cape of Good Hope Route.

THE SLAVE TRADE

In 1441, Henry sent a fleet south to Africa. It returned with 10 African prisoners. The slave trade had begun.

The Portuguese actually went ashore, kidnapped African people, and then forced them to work as slaves. One Portuguese explorer, Gomes Eannes de Azurar, described one of his early slave raids:

The Moors [Africans] having evidently had unfortunate experience with former white visitors, with their women and children were already coming as quickly as they could out of their houses, because they had caught sight of their enemies. But [the Portuguese], crying "St. James," "St. George," and "Portugal," attacked them at once, killing and taking all they could.

Skilled Benin bronzeworkers made this striking statue of a Portuguese slave hunter in around 1600. (British Museum)

This trade became so profitable that the Portuguese government actually began to license it, making it an officially recognized activity. Prince Henry himself greeted Azurara's return and rejoiced in the taking of 235 slaves. These slaves consisted of many different African peoples, for Azurara describes them as being light-skinned as well as dark-skinned.

Justifications. The Portuguese found it easy to justify slavery. The writer Joao De Barros said simply,

> [Slaves are] outside the law of Christ, and at the disposition, so far as their bodies were concerned, of any Christian nation.

Justified in this way, the slave trade developed into a huge enterprise. It destroyed many African peoples. On the African coast itself, Arabs soon joined the slave trade, capturing Africans to sell to the Europeans. Sometimes Africans would also capture fellow Africans from enemy tribes and sell them into slavery.

EXPLORING THE AFRICAN COAST

Portuguese Explorers. For a few years, the Portuguese focused on the slave trade. Then Henry's vision of world exploration prevailed. In 1455, two Genoese sailors whom he had sponsored went as far as the Gambia and Senegal rivers. This gave the Portuguese an opening into trade with the Sudan (the region south of the Sahara Desert).

In 1456, the same Genoese explorers discovered some islands off Cape Verde (the "Green Cape"), the westernmost point of Africa. The explorations continued. But by the time Henry died in 1460, they had only got as far down the West African coast as Sierra Leone. (The Portuguese named this area *leone*, the lion, because of the thunderstorms that always growled in the mountains.)

King Alfonso V of Portugal continued Henry's policy. He sponsored Lisbon trader Fernao Gomes to explore the African coast in exchange for a five-year monopoly on trade in the region known as Guinea.

The idea worked. During his five-year trade monopoly, Gomes rounded the bulge of West Africa and followed the coast due east as far as Benin. In the process he developed for the Portuguese some of the most profitable trade on the coast of West Africa.

The Portuguese named these West African regions after the goods found there. For example, in the region later known as Liberia a low-quality pepper was found, so it was (temporarily) called the Grain Coast. Beyond that was the Ivory Coast. Then came the Gold Coast (now the country of Ghana), where Gomes' expedition found gold in the streams.

Portugal Faces Competition. The Portuguese tried to keep their explorations secret, so that they would be the only ones to know about these rich trading areas. But merchants from other countries realized that the Portuguese had many new African goods. In the 1470s, Spanish, English, and Flemish ships all raided Portuguese settlements. (Flemish ships came from Flanders, which is now part of the country of Belgium.)

Portugal fought successfully to protect its African monopoly. Although Spain took some territory, Portugal kept most of the islands it had conquered, plus all fishing, trading, and navigation rights to West Africa.

New Explorations. Portugal continued its explorations in other parts of the world. When John II became king of Portugal in 1481, the Portuguese again began to try to find a sea route to India. Their movement down the west coast of Africa was very slow once they got below the equator; they were trying to sail south, but the winds and currents all ran north.

The Portuguese continued to believe that they had a right to rule the land and the people who lived there because they were Europeans and Christians. King John even initiated the use of *padroes*, stone columns topped by a cube and a cross. Explorers set these into the ground as they moved further along down the coast. The *padroes* were used as markers to signify that the land now belonged to Portuguese Christians.

The Portuguese were making fortunes from the profitable spice trade. However, they still faced hostility from the Moslem and African peoples they encountered. These people saw them as outsiders. The Portuguese kept working their way south, hoping to find some friendly kingdom where they could get food and a secure place to fix their ships before setting back for the long trip to Europe.

THE ACCIDENTAL DISCOVERY OF BARTHOLOMEU DIAS

This need drove explorer Batholomeu Dias further down the African coast in 1487. As they traveled south, Dias' party ran into extremely bad weather. For almost two weeks, a *gale*, or sea storm, followed them down the coast. The gale's waves were so high that, according to one sailor,

> ...as the ships were tiny, and the seas [cold]...they gave themselves up for dead.

This violent storm drove the sailors west, out away from the coast. Imagine how frightening it must have been, to be alone in the sea on a tiny boat, driven further and further away from land.

The early Portuguese fort of Sao Jorge da Mina in time became, in Dutch and later British hands, the stronghold of Elmina. (From de Bry, *Petits Voyages*, Part VI, Frankfurt, 1604)

Then the storm passed. Dias tried to go east looking for the coast. But for several days, he found no land. Finally, he headed north, and arrived in what is now Mossel Bay in South Africa, and which is east of the Cape of Good Hope. The storm had driven him past the southern tip of Africa without his even noticing it!

For several years, the Portuguese had been working their way down the west coast of Africa, never knowing how much further the giant continent extended. Now they had found out. Dias and his men took on fresh water and sailed back up the east coast of Africa. It was a difficult journey, for the currents flowed south and they were sailing north. Finally, Dias' sailors said they would go no farther and they turned south once more.

This time, there was no storm, so, since Dias' ships were hugging the coast, they had a sight of the southernmost tip of Africa, which they called Cape Agulhas.

The Cape of Good Hope. Just north of Cape Agulhas is another cape, which Dias named Cabo Tormentoso, or "Cape Stormy." But his king, John, is said to have renamed it the Cabo de Boa Esperanca, or the "Cape of Good Hope," because it promised good hope of a sea route to India. Certainly this cape was always a welcome sight to sailors later heading east, who knew when they saw it that they had finished a good part of their journey!

Vasco da Gama

Dias returned to Lisbon in 1488, and told the court of his important discovery. Even though he described the southern tip of Africa and the Cape of Good Hope, no new attempt to go forward was made until 1498.

The Renaissance. Many new changes had been taking place during these years. This period—the end of the 15th century—is generally called the Renaissance, which means "rebirth."

The Renaissance was a time of new ideas and discoveries. Scientists were saying that knowledge should be tested through experiments and observation, rather than relying on old untested principles and ideas.

In the same way, explorers were visiting places that were new to them. Instead of relying on the old maps, explorers were making new maps based on their own observations. They were driven by a scientific curiosity—and by the desire to find a way to get to India, where they could make their fortune bringing back the rare spices that only grew in the East. These explorers were also eager for the valuable Indian cottons, silks, jewels, and other ornaments, all of which were highly desirable in Europe.

One of the most important explorers was Christopher Columbus, an Italian sailor sponsored by King Ferdinand and Queen Isabella of Spain. Columbus knew that scientists had been claiming that the world was round. He believed that if he sailed west, he would end up in India, even though India was east of Spain. Actually, Columbus would have accomplished this—if he hadn't run into North and South America first.

Columbus' journey was very useful to other sailors. Not only did they learn that there was another world between them and India, they also learned much more about handling the Atlantic winds.

Da Gama Finds a New Route. Thus when Vasco da Gama set off to India in 1498, he tried a very different route than Bartholomeu Dias had. And in fact, da Gama developed a route that would become the standard way to travel the South Atlantic toward the Cape of Good Hope.

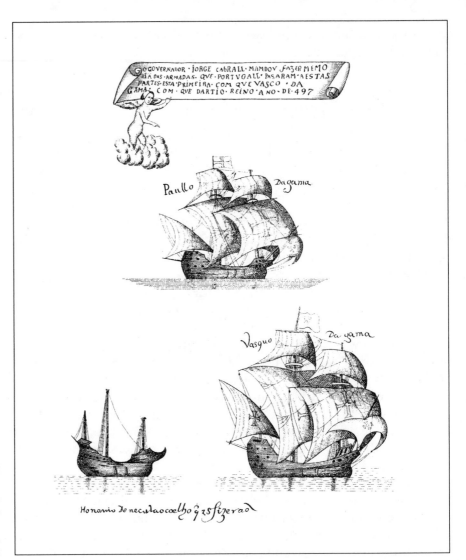

GO·GOVERNADOR ·JORGE·CABRALL· MAMDOV ·FAZER MEMO
RIA·DAS·ARMADAS· QVE·PORTVGALL· PASARAM·A ESTAS
PARTES·ESTA·PRIMEIRA· COM · QVE·VASCO · DA
GAMA· COM · QVE·DARTIO· REINO·A NO·DE·497

Paullo   Dagama

Vasquo   Da gama

Honario De necutaocoelho q̃ zs fizerad

Vasco da Gama opened up the Cape of Good Hope Route toIndia and the East sailing a square-rigged ship called *não*, shown here. (Science Museum, London)

From Lisbon da Gama passed through the Canary and Cape Verde islands. He took fresh water at Santiago (one of the Cape Verde Islands), then worked his way southeast. Finally, he found the trade winds that blew him southwest across the ocean, toward Brazil. When he had almost reached Brazil, another set of trade winds blew him back toward the southeast, so that he had in fact zig-zagged across the Atlantic, back to the Cape of Good Hope.

Brazil. Brazil itself was still unknown. All da Gama knew was that the winds were blowing him west, then east. He had no idea that if he had kept going west, he would have run into another continent. Brazil was not discovered by the Europeans until 1500, on another expedition toward India led by Pedro Cabral.

Vasco da Gama Finds the Spice Route

Da Gama himself ended up on the southeastern part of the African coast, as he had intended. His plan had been to round the Cape of Good Hope and then to head east to India. First, however, he had to find a friendly port where he could get food, fresh water, and other supplies. This proved to be difficult.

One day da Gama and his men came upon a merchant people on a bay they called Mozambique. One of the sailors described what they found:

> [The people here] are Mohammedans [Moslems], and their language is the same as that of the Moors [the North African Moslem people who had been living in Spain and Portugal]. Their dresses are of fine linen or cotton stuffs, with variously colored stripes, and of rich and elaborate workmanship. They all wear *toucas* [robes?] with borders of silk embroidered in gold. They are merchants, and have transactions with [other]...Moors, four of whose vessels were at the time in port, laden with gold, silver, cloves, pepper, ginger, and silver rings, as also with quantities of pearls, jewels, and rubies, all of which articles are used by the people of this country.

Da Gama had reached the southernmost port along the old Spice Route. The Spice Route was a network of sea routes that linked Southeast Asia, China, Africa, and the Middle East. For many years, the Spice Route had supplied goods to Europe by way of the Middle East, but Europeans themselves had not traveled this route. Now da Gama had discovered how to get to it. (For more about the Spice Route and the Europeans, see Chapter 3.)

The Portuguese and the Moslems. Not surprisingly, the Moslems did not take kindly to the Portuguese intruders. In their first contacts in Mozambique and Mombasa, the Portuguese and the Moslems at first followed the form of the time. The visiting commander sent ashore gifts for the local ruler, who also sent gifts in return.

But the Portuguese gifts were cheap goods—strips of cloth, scarlet hoods, coral necklaces. These were not good enough for the East African rulers, who draped themselves in silk, velvet, and gold.

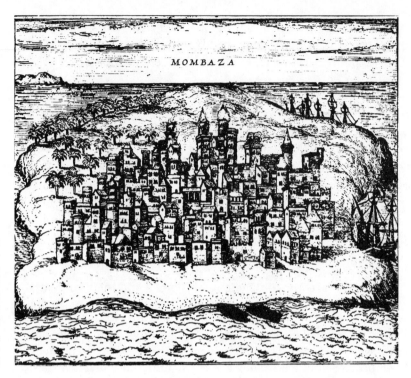

MOMBAZA

Mombasa, where da Gama's party was almost captured, later became a major port of contention among powers in the Indian Ocean. (From G. Braun and F. Hogenberg, *Civitates Orbis Terrarum*, Cologne, 1576)

More to the point, the Arabs realized that the Portuguese were possible rivals, both in trade and in religion. If they knew what had happened in Spain and Portugal in 1492, they would have been even more unfriendly. In that year, the Christian rulers Ferdinand and Isabella had thrown all the Moslems, or Moors, out of Spain. Portugal did the same thing. The Spanish also threw out all the Jews, hoping to make the country entirely Christian.

The Moslems in Africa feared that the Portuguese would cut into their trade, and began to plot to capture da Gama's party. Da Gama learned that there was a plot against him, and managed to get away just in time.

But the explorer still had to find a welcoming port. His crew was suffering badly from a disease called *scurvy*, which is caused by a lack of vitamins found in fresh fruits and vegetables, and he needed fresh water and more food.

Luckily for him, da Gama found Malindi, which was a rival port to Mombasa. The ruler of Malindi gave da Gama the safe haven and supplies he needed. Perhaps he would not have done so if he had known that da Gama was only the first of a series of European explorers. Now that the Europeans had connected with the Spice

Route, they would use their military power to take over much of its trade, as well as to conquer huge portions of Africa, Asia, and the Middle East to create colonies.

DA GAMA REACHES INDIA

An Experienced Pilot. The ruler of Malindi helped da Gama with more than supplies. He gave him a pilot, Ahmed ibn Majid, one of the leading navigators of the Indian Ocean. Ibn Majid was the author of some sailing books used by people in the East. Although all these routes were new to the Europeans, Indians, Moslems, and other Asians had been using them for centuries.

Ibn Majid shared this old knowledge with the Portuguese. He guided da Gama's expedition up the coast of East Africa and across the Arabian Sea. He also showed the crew how to catch fresh fish on the way.

Calicut, an Indian Port. Finally, ibn Majid guided da Gama to the southwest Indian port of Calicut. This was a good choice. A Moslem merchant had called this port "one of the greatest shipping centers of the world in this period." He also noted that the people of Calicut were "adventurous sailors, and pirates do not dare to attack" their ships. Not only could one find everything they desired in Calicut—they could count on their safety there.

Da Gama's crew played drums and trumpets and flew banners as they sailed into this great port. Their priests celebrated the end of this historic journey. Finally, Europeans had found a route to India.

As portrayed by a 16th-century European artist, Calicut was a prosperous, hospitable city. (From G. Braun and F. Hogenberg, *Civitates Orbis Terrarum*, Cologne, 1576)

However, da Gama's arrival was not a surprise to the rulers of the port. That's because the fast Arab *dhows*, or ships, had gotten there before him, bringing news of his arrival. The rulers of Calicut answered da Gama's greetings and sent a local pilot to show the ships to a safe anchorage. This was important, for soon would come the monsoons—the heavy winds and rainstorms of the southwestern Indian coast.

Negotiations with the Indians. Once da Gama's ship was safely anchored, he led a parade—including Portuguese bagpipes—through the streets of Calicut. The king who met him, however, did not receive him very warmly. Like the Africans and Moslems, he found the Portuguese gifts laughable, not nearly as good as his own country's products. Likewise, the trade goods of the Portuguese—mostly cloth and hardware—were far more crude than those normally traded in the region.

At this time, mainly Arab merchants carried goods out of India and into other parts of the East. The Calicut ruler did not see any

Da Gama and his crew probably saw sailors in small boats like these off India's southwest coast. (From de Bry, *Petits Voyages,* Part II, Frankfurt, 1599)

reason why he should trade with the Portuguese, who could not offer him goods as valuable or as necessary as those brought by the Arabs.

Finally, however, he made a small agreement with da Gama. The European goods might not have been of very high quality, but their weapons were the most powerful that had ever been seen. Perhaps the ruler felt he did not have much choice.

In any case, he gave da Gama a small amount of pepper and cinnamon, along with a letter to take to his king:

> Vasco da Gama, a nobleman of your household, has visited my kingdom and has given me great pleasure. In my kingdom there is abundance of cinnamon, cloves, ginger, pepper, and precious stones. What I seek from thy country is gold, silver, coral, and scarlet [cloth].

The king may have seemed polite, but local traders were openly hostile. Da Gama was concerned about this—so much so that he did not put his ships ashore and take them apart, even though they badly needed to be refitted and repaired.

Meanwhile, the ruler of Calicut tried to hold all the goods that the Portuguese had not yet sold, as payment for heavy port taxes. Da Gama did not want to pay the tax, or to lose his goods. He kidnapped some local people and held them hostage. The ruler eventually let him leave without him having to pay.

Monsoons. Da Gama left Calicut far too soon, as far as the monsoon season was concerned. It still had a month more to run, which caused the Portuguese great trouble crossing the Indian Ocean. They decided to stop at one of the many islands in the ocean, instead.

Finally, in late September, the winds changed. Now they blew from northeast to southwest—just what da Gama and his men needed to reach Africa again. They sailed back to friendly Malindi, where they were revived by fresh fruit and vegetables. Still, over one-third of them had died, mostly of scurvy.

The Return Home. As other sailors would find, the trip back around the Cape of Good Hope was fairly easy. Currents and winds carried them easily around the coast in the direction they wanted to go.

Remember that the trip south required sailors to zigzag far out into the Atlantic, away from Africa almost to Brazil. But on the return trip sailors encountered different currents, which allowed them to stay close to the coast. Vasco da Gama and his men arrived home 22 months after they had left.

Dominating the Spice Route

The Portuguese quickly made use of what da Gama had learned. For years they and other Europeans had dreamed of having access to the Spice Route, and of finding a sea route to India. Now that dream was within reach.

Within six months of da Gama's return, Pedro Cabral led a trading fleet along the same route. Heavy storms sank several ships, including one commanded by Bartholomeu Dias. But the rest of the voyage went smoothly.

However, the people of Calicut were not willing to trade with the Portuguese. So Cabral went further south on the Indian coast to another major port, Cochin. There he was permitted to build a factory (warehouse) for his trade goods.

Even with permission to trade, however, the Portuguese found that they could not compete with the Arab traders. So they decided to make war on them.

War with the Arabs and Indians. Da Gama himself returned to India in 1502. On his way, he demanded tribute or payment, from the rich East African trading city of Kilwa.

Then, when da Gama reached Calicut, he bombarded the city. He fought with both Indians and Arabs.

Other Portuguese soldiers and explorers followed da Gama. By 1513, they had taken all the key points along the Spice Route, including ports in India, Indonesia, and China. They forced "protection" payments from all, and attacked those who would not pay.

Once the Portuguese had taken control, they drove most of the Arabs out of the trade. The Cape of Good Hope Route took over from the Spice Route as the main path for spices to travel westward to Europe. And in less than 20 years, the Portuguese had become the main force in the Indian Ocean.

The Portuguese in Africa

The Portuguese were interested mainly in the Spice Route ports, but that didn't stop them from continuing to derive profits from Africa, as well. They had taken islands along the coast of West

On the long voyages around Africa to the East, the Portuguese lost many ships, like the São Thomé here in 1589. (From Bernardo Gomes de Brito, *Historia Tragico-maritima*, vol. II, Lisbon, 1735–6, British Museum)

Africa, and traded with cities along the coast. They also focused on the Congo and Angola, in southwest Africa; Mozambique (which they called "Portuguese East Africa"); and Abyssinia (which is called Ethiopia today).

The Portuguese took great numbers of slaves from the Congo and Angola. In Mozambique, they sought different kinds of riches. They believed that the legendary treasures of King Solomon were to be found in the city of Ophir.

The Africans, however, resisted strongly. They pushed the Portuguese out of some ports, including Kilwa. Only with the continued help of the Moslem rulers in Malindi did the Portuguese maintain control of the area.

The Portuguese connected Abyssinia with another myth. They had long believed that there was a Christian priest, called Prester John, who had set up a kingdom in this part of Africa. Although there was no Prester John, there were Christian believers in the land.

The Portuguese's interest in Abyssinia was not only to convert it totally to Christianity, they also wanted to take the Abyssinian port of Massawa, near the mouth of the Red Sea. They thought that taking this port would help them to control the Red Sea. But the Abyssinians resisted this, and won.

The Decline of Portugal. Portugal held on to its monopoly of the spice trade into the 1550s, but then it finally lost control to other European powers.

This decline had many causes. Portugal, a small country, had been hard hit by plague. It had also lost nine of every ten sailors that went abroad, either because the sailors died or because they stayed overseas.

Portuguese colonies abroad were constantly at war with local people and Moslem rivals. Finally and most importantly, Portugal itself was conquered by Spain in 1578.

EUROPEAN RIVALS

Other countries were beginning to trade in the Indian Ocean during the period of Portugal's decline. The French, the British, and the Dutch were all looking for their share of the profitable spice trade. These countries were fighting each other in European wars as well as competing for the best route to India.

In the late 1580s, the English defeated the Spanish Armada (the Spanish fleet). The Dutch also overthrew Spanish rule. Both the English and the Dutch were then ready to try the Cape of Good Hope Route.

Scurvy. The English and the Dutch had had no experience at all with the seas of the East, however. In addition, they faced an even more difficult problem—scurvy.

The disease of scurvy was caused by the lack of vitamin C, but this was not discovered until many years later. At this time sailors on long sea voyages had no access to fresh fruits or vegetables, which provide vitamin C, and so became sick with the disease. Jean Moquet, who sailed on the Cape of Good Hope Route during this period, describes some of his scurvy symptoms:

> It rotted all my gums, which gave out a black and putrid blood. My knee joints were so swollen that I could not extend my muscles. My thighs and lower legs were black and gangrenous [gangrene is a disease that rots the flesh], and I was forced to use my knife each day to cut into the flesh in order to release this black and foul blood....And the unfortunate thing was that I could not eat...because of my great suffering....Many of our people died of it every day, and we saw bodies being thrown into the sea constantly, three or four at a time....On every side were heard only the cries of those assailed by

thirst, hunger, and pain, cursing the hour when they had come aboard....

Scurvy was so dangerous that in these years, ships were sometimes found drifting in the open sea with most of their crew dead. The few survivors were often too weak to run the ship.

Some ships had to return when few of their crew remained. Others were broken up or burned aboard, for there were too few sailors to man them. The northern Europeans had even more serious problems with scurvy than the Portuguese, since they had longer journeys to make because they were starting from points further north.

Problems of the English Sailors. Besides facing the dangers of scurvy, the English had other problems dealing with this long voyage around Africa. Their ships were not properly prepared for tropical waters. They needed double sheathing—two layers of boards covering the ship's hull—in order to protect the ship from rot. Because of their inexperience, however, the English did not know this.

The English also did not have good ports along the way. There was nowhere they could go for the supplies they needed during their trip.

These problems were so severe that the first English attempt to reach India failed. The second expedition reached the island of Mauritius—but with only one sailor surviving.

Skills of the Dutch. The Dutch did a little better, partly because they were better prepared. The Dutch had taken part in East Indian trade for some time. Because the Portuguese were such a small nation, they had needed help from the Dutch. Merchants from the Netherlands had financed Portugal's expeditions. The Netherlands also had the main market—Antwerp— where the Portuguese had brought their Eastern goods.

Because of this connection, some Dutch sailors had sailed on a Portuguese ship to the East Indies in 1595 and 1596. One had written navigational guides to the routes—even though the Portuguese had wanted to keep these routes secret.

The Dutch in Java. So the Dutch made a successful voyage in 1596, landing in Java, in the present-day country of Indonesia. The company that had sent them was called the "Company for Distant

Lands." They hoped to trade, but did not know how they would be greeted.

They could not have been welcomed more warmly. Local nobles and other leaders crowded on board to greet them, as did merchants from many other countries:

> There came such a multitude of Javanese and other nations as Turks, Chinese, Bengali, Arabs, Persians, Gujarati [from a region of India], and others that one could hardly move....they...came so abundantly that each nation took a spot on the ships where they displayed their goods, the same as if it were on a market. Of which the Chinese brought...all sorts of silk woven and unwoven, twined and untwined, with beautiful earthenware, with other strange things more. The Javanese brought chickens, eggs, ducks, and many kinds of fruits, Arabs, Moors, Turks, and other nations of people each brought of everything one might imagine....

After this warm welcome, however, the Javanese became suspicious of the Dutch. They even imprisoned some of them.

Eventually, however, the Dutch made a trade agreement with the Javanese and took some profitable goods home with them. Three out of their four ships returned safely—a record in those days—but two-thirds of the crew had died, mostly of scurvy.

The Dutch were disturbed by this high death rate. They tried another sea route, the Cape Horn Route, around South America and across the Pacific. But this route was even worse.

The Dutch continued to journey along the Cape of Good Hope Route, establishing themselves further in Java. Finally, by 1599, the Portuguese were too weak to keep the Dutch out. The Dutch then focused on the eastern end of the Spice Route, especially the Molucca Islands and Java. In 1602, they founded the Dutch East India Company to trade in the region.

The British Move East. The British formed their own East India Company in 1600. Just as the Dutch had been helped by their contact with the Portuguese, so were the British helped by their contact with the Dutch. John Davis, a British pilot, was on the 1599 Dutch voyage. Of course, neither the Portuguese nor the Dutch wanted to help their rivals!

The first British voyage around the Cape of Good Hope in 1601 was unusual. The sailors on one ship were given lemon juice and, unlike the others, they did not get scurvy. We now know that this

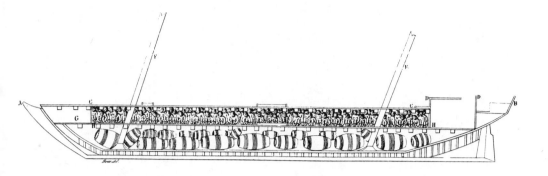

is because lemon juice contains vitamin C, but this was not yet understood. It would take Britain 200 more years to require that all its sailors be given citrus juices. That's how British sailors got the nickname "limeys."

Like the Dutch, the British headed for the Spice Islands. Together, the British and the Dutch captured a Portuguese ship in 1602, and this was the beginning of Portugal's gradual loss of control.

Portuguese Defeats. Portugal did have some victories in keeping its Spice Island ports, but gradually other Europeans became dominant along the Spice Route.

Portugal also lost many of its colonies on the west coast of Africa. In the 1630s, the Dutch took many of the rich ports on the Guinea Coast. They also took Angola, although the Portuguese later reclaimed it.

The Portuguese did keep control of the poor ports near Bissau. They also kept control of the part of the coast that ran down from Sao Tome Island down to the Cape of Good Hope. With this territory, they were able to keep up their active slave trade with Brazil.

The Founding of South Africa. The Cape of Good Hope continued to be a watering and rest stop for all European ships. No one country was able to lay claim to this important area.

Then, in 1648, a ship was shipwrecked on the cape. "Cape Stormy" *had* been an accurate name for this area! While the crew waited to be rescued, they planted crops in order to survive.

As a result, in 1652, the Dutch settled a colony at the cape. They thought a colony could provide fresh fruits and vegetables for Dutch sailors on the long-distance runs to the East. This settlement was the beginning of the enslavement of many native Africans.

The slave trade from Africa lasted for centuries; this early 19th-century Spanish ship, *La Josefa Maracayera*, off the Bay of Benin, packed over 200 black African slaves with sacks of rice. (Bibliothèque Nationale, Paris)

East India sailing ships left the Netherlands with their flags flying in the great days of the Cape of Good Hope Route. (By Hendrick Cornelisz Vroom, Rijksmuseum, Amsterdam)

DUTCH TRADING IN THE AGE OF PIRATES

During this period, the Dutch seemed to be the greatest European power in the East. They had learned much from the Portuguese, and had added some new knowledge of their own. They discovered a new route across the Indian Ocean that cut one year off a fleet's round-trip. This new route was not only faster, but it also bypassed the area when the monsoons struck.

In addition, Dutch ships were easier to handle than other European boats in the Indian Ocean. The Dutch were also well organized. They handled all their activities from a single head-quarters at Djakarta on the island of Java (today Jakarta is the capital of the present-day country of Indonesia). In accordance with European practice at the time, they renamed the cities they found: they called Jakarta "Batavia."

Rivalry. The Dutch did not control the whole of the Cape of Good Hope Route. From the mid-17th to the mid-18th century, no one power really ruled the seas, as the Portuguese had the century before. Instead, many rivals fought each other, including the Portuguese, the Arabs, the Dutch, the British, the French, the Danes, and the many peoples of Southeast Asia.

Pirates. Some historians call this period the "Age of Pirates," after the huge numbers of pirates who sailed the Indian Ocean. Many of

these were the kinds of pirates who had sailed the old Spice Route for centuries, attacking ships and stealing their cargoes. Other pirates had come from other parts of the world, taking advantage of this rich territory.

By the early 17th century, the problem had become quite serious. Even rivals like the English and the Dutch sometimes sailed together in convoys for protection.

By the late 17th century, the problem was even more serious. At that time, many pirates had been forced out of the Caribbean. They came over to Madagascar, off the coast of Africa, and used it as a base from which they could sail the Indian Ocean.

These freebooters were from many countries, but most of them were English. They grew so bold, they even set up their own republic on Madagascar, which they named Libertalia.

Americans from New York, Boston, and Philadelphia first appeared on the Cape of Good Hope Route during this period. Around 1700, they were acting as merchants to Madagascar—supplying the community of pirates! Among these was the famous Captain Kidd, who was supposed to possess a treasure taken partly from a haul he made in the Indian Ocean.

Madagascar and other nearby islands were favored watering spots and pirates' haunts, so fortified villages grew along the coastline. (By Van Linschoten, 1609, Bibliothèque Nationale)

Captain Kidd was known and feared by many. A *chief factor*, or merchant's agent, on the southwest coast of India, described the pirate like this:

> This captain is very severe to his people...procuring his awe and respect from his men, and to this is added his own strength, being a very lusty man often calling for his pistols, and threatening any that durst [dares] speak to the contrary of what he desireth, to knock out their brains....They are a very distraited company, continually quarreling and fighting among themselves....We were informed that...in Madagascar is settled great abundance of these villainous people with their families, yearly supplied from New York with liquors, provisions, and other goods....

Gradually, the European trading companies managed to subdue the pirates. They armed their trading ships more heavily. They also attracted—or forced—pirates to join law-abiding settlements in the region.

COMPETITION AMONG THE EUROPEANS

The Decline of Dutch Power. By the mid-18th century, Britain and France dominated the Cape of Good Hope Route. The Dutch were much weaker, for they had lost their colonies in North America.

By this time, too, ship sizes had grown—but the Dutch home ports in the Netherlands could only handle fairly small ships. The English now had big ships, called "the East Indiamen," which they used in the East.

Interestingly, the Dutch had encouraged their traders to bring their wives and families at first to their settlements overseas, but later they changed their policy and encouraged their traders to marry local people. The only place the Dutch maintained a separate settlement was at Cape Town, their colony on the Cape of Good Hope. South Africa today still has laws against Dutch descendants marrying native Africans.

The Rise of the British. As Dutch power declined, the fortunes of the British rose. In West Africa, these two nations pushed out the Portuguese and Spanish and took over the slave trade.

Further east, in India, the British were especially strong. Their main Indian port was Surat. This city was so rich that some of the streets were paved in porcelain.

The French had some bases in Africa and India, but were not nearly as powerful as the British. The British were gradually taking over India, as the Indian trade grew ever more profitable. In the late 18th century, the British continued to expand, while the Dutch and French East India Companies both had financial trouble, and many of Portugal's trading ships were rotting in their harbors.

In 1789, the French people revolted against the French upper classes in what is called the French Revolution, overthrowing the monarchy and setting up a republic in its place. This was a huge upheaval, and led to many civil wars in France. With the French preoccupied with matters at home, they could not spare the resources to continue to conquer other peoples.

After the French Revolution, a soldier named Napoleon rose to power. The French Republic did not last very long, and Napoleon eventually made himself emperor. He conquered many countries in Europe, and also tried to regain France's power in the Indian Ocean. But Napoleon lost the key battle of Waterloo to the British and Prussians in 1815 and fell from power.

Many East India Company ships were built in the East of hard Asian wood, like the *Earl of Balcarras* built of teak in Bombay in 1815. (Science Museum, London)

Landing in the Bay of Tolaga, New Zealand, October 23-9, 1769. New Zealand is a neighbor of Australia. (By Captain James Cook, after Parkinson, British Museum)

When the British gained dominance in Europe (after the battle of Waterloo), they gained power in the East as well. By 1815, they had driven both the Dutch and the French from India and Ceylon (today, Sri Lanka), and were also strong in Malaya (present-day Malaysia).

The British had tried twice to take the Cape of Good Hope from the Dutch, and the second time they succeeded. Thus the country of South Africa is inhabited by descendants of Dutch and British settlers.

THE ERA OF BRITISH RULE

The British had also gained control of a whole new continent—Australia. This rich land had been claimed for England in 1770 when Captain James Cook sailed into Botany Bay. Captain Cook's ship had been traveling on the Cape of Good Hope Route, but it had been blown off course towards Australia!

At first, the British colonized Australia with convicts alone. Instead of sending them to jail in Britain, they sent them out of the country to Australia, where they became farmers or worked in other ways. Just as the British settlers in America found native peoples with their own culture and civilization, so did the settlers in Australia. The native peoples there are called *aborigines*.

Convicts were sent to Australia for decades. Even so, by the mid-19th century, the European population of Australia numbered only about 5,000 people. The rough land and the convict society did not attract many others from Britain.

Likewise, the Cape of Good Hope colony—ancestor of present-day South Africa—did not attract many British. The land there was fruitful, but most of the Europeans living there were the Dutch-speaking farmers called *Boers*. British citizens who wanted to make their fortunes in other lands went mostly to Canada, instead.

Gold and Diamonds

However, in 1851, gold was discovered in New South Wales, in Australia. Suddenly Australia became a very popular place to be! In 1871 diamonds were discovered in the Cape Colony, and in 1886 gold was discovered there too. Now people from all over the world were coming to Australia and South Africa to seek their fortunes.

Speed in sailing ships became a prime factor, as Europeans raced to get to the gold and diamonds before anybody else. New, faster

In the great days of the "tea runs"—when ships carried Chinese tea to England—these clippers raced from China to London. (By Edwin Weeden, from *The Illustrated London News*, September 9, 1866)

ships were built. Navigators also knew more about the Atlantic and its trade winds, and were able to take more direct routes than they had in the past. Soon, the new *clipper* ships were making the trip from England to Australia in as little as 65 days.

Speed was more important in the Far East, too. As Europe entered the industrial age, two years became far too long for the usual round trip to the Far East. For many years, the Ottoman Empire of the Turks had held much land in the Middle East, making it difficult for Europeans to cross overland. By the mid-19th century, Turkish power had declined. Europeans began going to Asia overland by rail instead of by sea.

All these developments sharply cut traffic on the Cape of Good Hope Route. Suddenly the southwest part of the Indian Ocean was a backwater. Traffic in that area was mainly aimed at the Cape Colony, Australia, and other islands off the South Pacific.

SAILING TO AUSTRALIA

Even though ships may have been faster during this period, they were still a difficult means of transportation. Before the discovery of gold, most passengers to Australia were convicts, and they were jammed together in prison ships.

After gold was found, many more immigrants went to Australia to seek their fortunes, but they didn't travel under conditions much better than the convicts had on the way over. Sailing historian Philip McCutchan describes the journey like this:

> ...the 'tween-decks [between the decks, where the cheapest accommodations were found] were like dungeons, dark and hot at times, dark and cold at others, and almost always wet. The straw beds rotted with the constant ingress [entry] of seawater; the passengers, many of them sick and all of them dispirited and weakened by prolonged poor feeding, could all too often not stir themselves to go on deck to perform their natural functions; preferring to remain *in situ* [in place] for the purpose. The result was a fearful [amount]...of steam and stench whenever the hatches were opened up above their suffering heads....

Travelers also had to prepare their own food. But illness and bad weather kept many from doing even that. Some passengers were undernourished; others actually starved. The death rates on these voyages were often as high as 50 to 100 deaths per trip.

These passengers, being held for quarantine off the Cape Verde Islands, are buying fresh food from enterprising local traders. (Bibliothèque Nationale, Paris)

The lure of gold drove people on even under these difficult conditions. Once ships arrived in Australia, their crews might desert so they, too, could join the rush for gold. British officers often forced people out of local jails and onto their ships just to get crews for the voyage home. They had to stand armed and alert for the whole voyage, to make sure these crews did not turn the ship around and go back to Australia.

After the Gold Rush. Gradually, the gold rush ended. But Australia still had an important product to send to Britain—wool.

The Australian climate and terrain were particularly suitable for raising sheep. Cattle ranches were also introduced in the late 1800s and Australia began to export meat. Still later, Australian vegetables were sent to England. The neighboring colony of New Zealand also joined in the trade.

The End of the Sailing Ship

During the 19th century, new types of ships were introduced—iron ships, steel ships, and finally, steamships. These ships, driven by coal-burning engines, were not practical on the long Cape of Good Hope Route because they required too much coal to make the journey.

The Suez Canal. But then, in 1869, a new development took place. A European company dug a canal through Egypt, connecting the Mediterranean with the Red Sea. (See Chapter 3.) Suddenly it was possible to travel between Europe and Asia much more quickly than ever before.

With this new route, sailing ships fell into disuse. These ships could not sail through the cnaal; they had to be towed, which was expensive. They also had trouble with the Red Sea winds.

Steamships had none of these troubles. By the 1880s, they had taken over the passenger trade and much of the cargo trade. Only the bulk cargo trade like grain and coal, was carried on sailing ships on round-the-world routes. However, after 1914, most of these ships went via the Panama Canal route.

The Cape of Good Hope Route Today

In modern time, the Cape of Good Hope Route still has some importance. The era of sailing ships has long ended, and most people prefer to travel by airplane. However, modern ships continue to haul heavy cargo from the ports of Africa, Australia, and New Zealand. Anything that is too heavy or expensive to carry by plane goes by ship.

In 1956, the fighting between Egypt and Israel led to the closing of the Suez Canal for a time. During that period, huge supertankers were developed to carry oil—and these ships were too big to use the canal once it was reopened, and so had to resort to the Cape of Good

Hope Route. Today, the old Cape of Good Hope Route is the lifeline along which flows the Western countries' precious oil.

Suggestions for Further Reading

Hart, Henry Hersch. *Sea Route to the Indies: An Account of the Voyages and Exploits of the Portuguese Navigators* (New York: Macmillan, 1950).

Howe, Sonia E. *In Quest of Spices* (London: Herbert Jenkins Ltd., 1939).

McCutchan, Philip. *Tall Ships: The Golden Age of Sail* (New York: Crown, 1976).

Parry, J. W. *The Age of Reconnaissance: Discovery, Exploration and Settlement 1450 to 1650* (New York: Praeger, 1969).

————. *Trade and Dominion: The European Overseas Empires in the Eighteenth Century* (New York: Praeger, 1971).

Penrose, Boies. *Travel and Discovery in the Renaissance: 1420–1620* (New York: Atheneum, 1975; reprint of Harvard University Press edition).

Tavernier, Bruno. *Great Maritime Routes: An Illustrated History* (London: MacDonald, 1972).

Van Leur, J. C. *Indonesian Trade and Society: Essays in Asian Social and Economic History* (The Hague: W. van Hoeve Ltd., 1955).

INDEX

L

Language and Linguistics 4, 6-7, 11, 28, 45-46, 54
Lesseps, Ferdinand Marie, vicomte de 60
Liaodong (peninsula) 67
Lighthouses 19
Limeys (British sailors) 97
Lintin Islands 55
Locks 61

M

Macao (Portuguese colony) 44, 48, 51, 55, 72
Mace 33
Madagascar (island) 1, 13, 77, *99*
Magellan, Ferdinand 45
Majid, Ahmed ibn 89
Malacca, Strait of 24
Malacca (Malay peninsular region) 32, 44, 47, 54
Malay Archipelago (East Indies) 2, 17, 48
Malay Peninsula 17, 31
Maldive Islands 32
Malindi (port) 29, 42, 88-89, 91
Manchuria 67
Manila (city) 45, 48, 58
Manuel I, King (Emanuel I) (Portugal) 42-43
Marathas (Hindu group) 49
Massawa (port) 93
Mauritius 77, 95
McCutchan, Philip 104
Mecca (Islamic holy city) 39
Mediterranean Sea
  Spice Route and 1
  Suez Canal and 9, 53, 60
Melukkha (city) 4
Mesopotamia
  Cape of Good Hope Route and 44
  Islam and 26
  Persia and 20
  Shipbuilding and 7
  Slave trade and 30
  Spice Route and 4, 44
Metalworkers 66
Mexico 45, 58
Mines and Mining 66-67
Ming Dynasty (China) 36-38, 46
Missionaries 21, 46, 65
Mogadishu (city) 29, 37
Mohammed (Arab prophet) 25-26, 29, 39, 77
Moluccas—*See Spice Islands*
Mombasa (port) 43, 48-49, 87, *88*
Mongols (Asian people) 33-34
Monsoon Winds 2-3, 16, 90-91
Moors (ancient people) 78, 80, 88
Moquet, Jean 94
Morocco 79
Moses (Hebrew prophet) 26

Moslems—*See Islam*
Mosques *25*
Mozambique 43, 48-49, 72, 87, 93
Muggs (pirates) 48
Muscat (city) 49, 64
Musk 29
Muziris (port) 16
Myanmar—*See Burma*
Myrrh 5, 12

N

Nabobism 63-64
Nagasaki (port) 58
Nanhai (city) 12, 20
Nao (ship) *86*
Napoleon I—*See Bonaparte, Napoleon*
Navigation 6, *39*
  Cape of Good Hope Route and 104
  China and 38
  Compass and 38-39
  of Indian Ocean 89
  Islam and 38-39
  of Spice Route 10, 16-17
  by the Stars 38-39
Nazi Germany 70-71
Nearchus (Macedonian general) 14-15
Netherlands, The
  China and 51
  France and 53
  Independence movements and 72
  Japan and 50, 52, 57-58
  Pirates and 98-100
  Scurvy and 94-96
  Shipbuilding and 98
  South Africa and 97
  Spice Route and 46, 48, 50-52, 63, 67
New Zealand 106
Nile River 9, 15
Noah (Biblical ark builder) 26
'Ntyw (Egyptian trade item) 5
Nutmeg 33, 50

O

Oil—*See Petroleum*
Oil Tankers 71
Oman and Omanis 29, 49
Ophir (city) 93
Opium Wars 54-57
Ormuz (port) *8*, 37, 43, 47, 49
Ottoman Empire 70, 104

P

Pacific Ocean 45, 58, 61
Padroes (Portuguese stone markers) 83
Palembang (city) 33
Palestine 73
Palm Oil 17

Panama Canal 61, 106
Parthia (ancient Asian country) 18
Peacocks 6
Pearl Harbor 70
Pearls 19, 87
Pemba (town) 29, 49, 51
Peninsular & Oriental Liner *66*
Peppers 19, *35*, 50, 82, 87, 91
Periplus of the Erythraean Sea (guidebook) 16
Perry, Matthew 58
Persian Empire
  Cape of Good Hope Route and 44
  China and 28
  Islam and 26
  Slave trade and 30
  Spice Route and 13, 20
Persian Gulf
  Alexander the Great and 14
  Cape of Good Hope Route and 44
  Cheng Ho and 37-38
  Islam and 26
  Jews and 31
  Navigation of 8, 16
  Pirates and 49
  Spice Route and 1, 4, 20
Petroleum
  Cape of Good Hope Route and 75, 106-107
  Spice Route and 71
  World War I and 68-69
Philippine Islands 45-46, 67, 71
Phoenicians 76-77
Physics 41
Pilgrims and Pilgrimages
  Buddhism and 24-25, 39
  I-Ching 27
  Islam and 39-40
Pirates and Piracy *36*, 98-100
  Age of 98-100
  China and 35-36
  Islam and 26, 35-36
  of Malay Peninsula 17
  Portugal and 44-45
  South China Sea and 44
  Spice Route and 26, 48-49
  Srivijaya Empire and 24
Plantations 66-67
Pliny the Elder 13
Polo, Marco 34-35
Porcelains 51
Portage 18, 21
Port Said (city) 60
Portugal
  Africa and 64, 79-80, 92-94
  Cape of Good Hope Route and 78-94, 97
  Exploration and 41-43, 78-79
  Henry the Navigator 78-79
  India and 42-44
  Islam and 43, 87-89